made for
Baby

❀ made for ❀
Baby

More than 50 fabulous gifts for babies

LONDON, NEW YORK, MUNICH,
MELBOURNE, DELHI

DK UK

Project Editor Kathryn Meeker
Senior Art Editor Nicola Rodway
Editor Hilary Mandelberg
Managing Editor Penny Smith
Senior Managing Art Editor Marianne Markham
Art Director for Photography Jane Ewart
Photographer Ruth Jenkinson
Jacket Designer Rosie Levine
Producer, Pre-Production Sarah Isle
Senior Producer Alex Bell
Creative Technical Support Sonia Charbonnier
Art Director Jane Bull
Publisher Mary Ling

DK INDIA

Senior Editor Dorothy Kikon
Senior Art Editor Ira Sharma
Assistant Art Editor Sourabh Challariya
Managing Editor Alicia Ingty
Managing Art Editor Navidita Thapa
Pre-Production Manager Sunil Sharma
Production Manager Pankaj Sharma
Senior DTP Designer Jagtar Singh

First published in Great Britain in 2014
by Dorling Kindersley Limited,
80 Strand, London, WC2R 0RL

Copyright © 2014 Dorling Kindersley Limited
A Penguin Random House Company

10 9 8 7 6 5 4 3 2 1

001–186489–Feb/2014

A CIP catalogue record for this book
is available from the British Library
ISBN 978-1-4093-7591-3

Printed and bound in China by South China Printing Co. Ltd.

Discover more at www.dk.com/crafts

Introduction

Having a new baby is the most exciting time and often prompts the desire to hand-make gorgeous gifts. *Made for Baby* shows you how to make beautiful clothing and toys for baby, accessories for the nursery, and keepsakes for mum that are sure to be cherished for many years.

This book contains more than 50 project ideas to inspire you. You can follow the steps closely, or use the general techniques to create your own projects. For example, try changing the shape of the ears and tail on the Floppy mouse toy (see pages 136–143) to make him into a rabbit; create your own stencil, stamp, or embroidery designs; or transform a simple hand drawing into a piece of appliqué or button art using the step-by-step techniques. Use your creativity to make each project your very own.

It is usually best to pre-wash and pre-shrink all fabrics for any project before cutting or sewing so when you wash the item in the future the fabrics will not shrink and distort your creation. Always be safety conscious when making anything for a baby or child and ensure that all pieces, especially buttons, are securely attached. Regularly check any handmade projects for wear and tear and repair them if necessary. Now all you have to do is turn the page to find the perfect gift for your special baby.

Contents

Nursery

ALSO NEEDED FOR THE LAMB

✿ Light-grey, black, and pink thread

✿ 25 x 30cm (9¾ x 12in) light-grey fabric for the body

✿ Scraps of cream and pink fabrics for the nose and bow

ALSO NEEDED FOR THE GIRAFFE

✿ Light-brown thread

✿ 30 x 20cm (12 x 8in) light-brown fabric for the body

✿ Scraps of light-brown fabric for the hooves, nose, forelock, and horns

Cuddly cushions

These lovable cushion covers make a charming set or can be used individually. Choose fabrics that complement each other but are different. Each cushion cover opens at the back to accommodate a 40 x 40cm (16 x 16in) cushion pad.

YOU WILL NEED ✿ marker pen or pencil ✿ tracing paper ✿ scissors ✿ 40 x 40cm (16 x 16in) fusible interfacing, per cushion ✿ fabrics for the animals (see opposite) ✿ iron ✿ pins ✿ 42 x 42cm (16½ x 16½in) square main cushion fabric and two 42 x 31cm (16½ x 12¼in) rectangles main cushion fabric, per cushion ✿ contrasting thread for tacking ✿ needle ✿ thread to match main cushion fabric ✿ sewing machine capable of zigzag stitch ✿ black embroidery thread ✿ large-eyed needle ✿ 45 x 45cm (17¾ x 17¾in) wadding, per cushion ✿ 45 x 45cm (17¾ x 17¾in) thin, white cotton fabric, per cushion

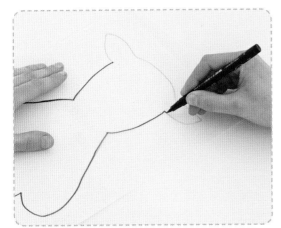

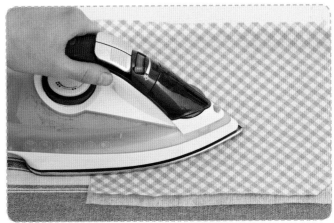

1 **With a marker pen or pencil,** trace the templates on page 228 for the lamb and giraffe onto the tracing paper. Cut out the templates.

2 **Iron the fabric for the animal's body** and the scraps for the animal details to the fusible interfacing, setting your iron to warm, not hot. Cut the fusible interfacing as required before you start. Make sure the shiny side of the interfacing is against the wrong side of the fabric. Press firmly on the iron until the fabric and interfacing have fused together.

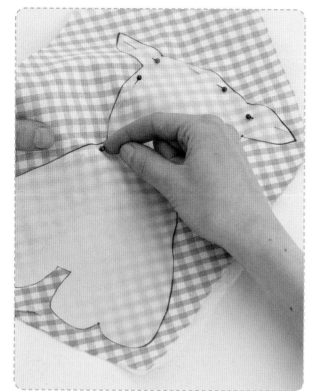

4 **Centre and pin the animal's body** on the front cushion fabric. If making the lamb, lay the bow and nose on top of the lamb's body. If making the giraffe, lay the hooves, nose, and forelock on top of the body and tuck the two horns slightly underneath the head. Pin all the pieces in place.

3 **Pin your template** pieces to their corresponding pieces of interfaced fabric. Cut around the templates, then remove the pins and the templates. Iron the main fabric square and the two rectangles. These will form the front and back flaps of the cushion respectively.

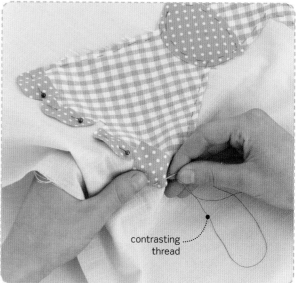

contrasting thread

5 **Using the contrasting thread,** tack all the pieces in place on the front cushion fabric. Tack around the edges of every piece, however small. Remove the pins.

6 **Set your sewing machine** to a wide zigzag stitch with a short 0-1 stitch length, to create a close satin stitch. Thread your sewing machine and bobbin with the correct colour thread and carefully stitch along all the edges of your pieces. (See the box, right, for more information.)

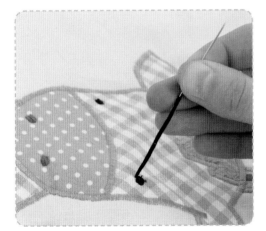

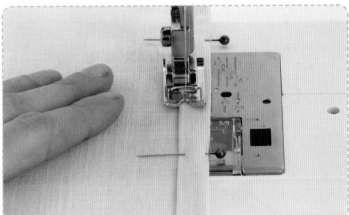

7 **Once your animal** is machine-stitched in place, remove all the tacking stitches. Thread the large-eyed needle with black embroidery thread and embroider the animals' eyes. The giraffe also has nostrils; use light-brown thread to embroider these.

8 **Hem one long edge** on each of the back flaps by folding it over twice, each time by 1cm (½in). Pin in place as shown. Thread your sewing machine and bobbin with matching thread and re-set the machine to a straight stitch of normal width and length. Stitch close to the edge of the fold. Remove the pins. Repeat on the second flap. Next, cut a piece of wadding and a piece of thin, white cotton, each 42 x 42cm (16½ x 16½in) square.

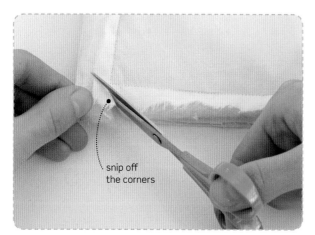

sandwich
the wadding
between the
white cotton
and cushion
front fabric

9 **Place the white cotton** on your work surface and top
it with the wadding. Top that with the cushion front,
right side up. Place one of the back flaps on top,
right side down, aligning its unhemmed edge with the
bottom edge of the cushion. Place the other back flap
on top, right side down, aligning its unhemmed edge
with the top edge of the cushion. The back flaps will
overlap. Pin the layers of fabric together around all four
sides of the cushion, aligning the edges.

snip off
the corners

10 **Machine along the four sides** of the cushion cover
using a 1cm (½in) seam allowance. Snip diagonally
across the four corners to remove the excess fabric,
taking care not to cut through the stitches. Turn
the cushion cover right side out and iron if needed.
Insert the cushion pad through the back.

TOP TIP *Don't touch the shiny side of the interfacing with the iron as it will stick to it.*

Keepsake handprint

Capture your baby's tiny handprint forever. This project is best done when baby is more than four months old. Before then her hand will close when you touch it, making it difficult to get a clear handprint.

YOU WILL NEED ✿ water-based non-toxic paint in the colour of your choice ✿ paintbrush ✿ watercolour paper ✿ craft knife ✿ ruler ✿ cutting mat ✿ scissors ✿ 33 x 33cm (13 x 13in) patterned fabric, or large enough to fit the frame ✿ masking tape ✿ double-sided tape ✿ 25 x 25cm (10 x 10in) frame, or the size of your choice

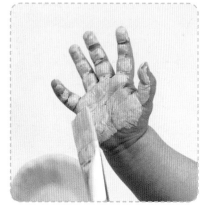

1 **Apply the paint** to your baby's hand using a paintbrush. Gently press her hand on the watercolour paper to make a print. Repeat the process, if necessary, until you have a clear print you are happy with. Wash the paint off your baby's hand and leave the handprint to dry.

2 **Using a craft knife,** ruler, and cutting mat, trim the watercolour paper so the handprint is centred within a square. Leave approximately 2.5cm (1in) of white space around the print. Make sure the square of paper is smaller than the frame by approximately 5cm (2in) so that the fabric will form a background to the handprint.

3 **Cut the fabric** to the size of the frame's backing board, adding approximately 2.5cm (1in) extra all round. Wrap the excess fabric around the backing board and stick it to the back with masking tape.

4 **Centre the handprint** over the patterned fabric, stick it down using double-sided tape, then place the completed project in the frame.

Night-sky mobile

Simple but adorable, this stars, clouds, and man-in-the-moon mobile made from soft, padded felt shapes is a classic addition to any nursery. Make sure to hang your mobile well out of baby's reach to avoid accidents: mobiles are not toys and you should always supervise your baby to avoid any accidents.

YOU WILL NEED ❀ tracing paper ❀ pencil or marker pen ❀ scissors ❀ pins
❀ 30.5 x 43cm (12 x 17in) yellow felt ❀ 38 x 43cm (15 x 17in) white felt ❀ large-eyed needle
❀ yellow, white, and grey embroidery thread ❀ toy filling
❀ a circular mobile frame or a painted stick, to hang the shapes from

1 **Trace the templates** on page 234 onto the tracing paper and cut them out to make the pattern pieces.

2 **Pin the pattern pieces** to the correct pieces of felt and cut them out. Cut out a total of eight yellow stars, two white moons, six small white clouds, and two large white clouds.

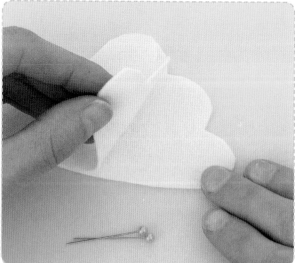

4 **Pin the felt pieces together** in pairs. You should have one moon with a face on either side, four stars, three small clouds, and one large cloud.

3 **Using the embroidery guides** on the templates on page 234, grey embroidery thread, and a large-eyed needle, embroider the man-in-the-moon's face on the first moon. Embroider a mirror image of the face on the second moon so that when you stitch the two moons together, your moon will have both sides of the face.

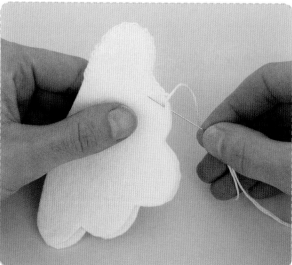

5 **Using blanket stitch** (see p.224) and matching embroidery thread, stitch together the edges of all the shapes, leaving a 2.5cm (1in) hole in the bottom of each through which you can stuff them. Remove the pins as you work.

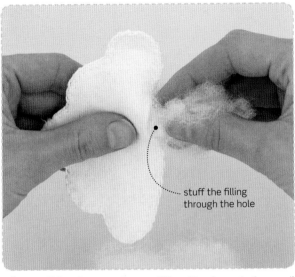

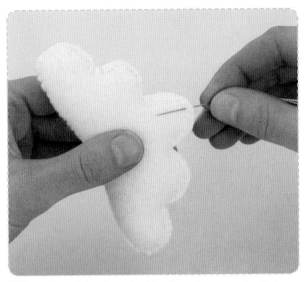

6 **Stuff the shapes** using toy filling. Use the end of a pencil to work the filling into all the corners, such as the points of the stars. Use blanket stitch to sew up the hole.

stuff the filling through the hole

7 **Using white thread** with a knot in one end, stitch through the top of each shape. Leave a long tail of thread for the shape to hang from.

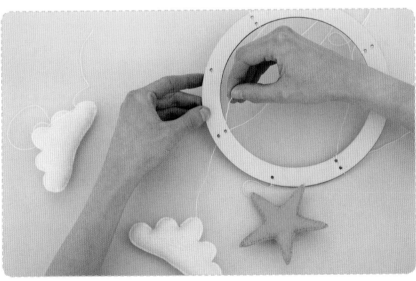

TIP
Hide any knots between the two halves of felt.

8 **Arrange the shapes around** the mobile frame and tie them securely in place. Mobile frames with pre-drilled holes are available from craft shops but you might like to hang the shapes from a painted twig instead. Use a piece of thread or ribbon to hang the finished mobile safely out of baby's reach.

Heirloom patchwork quilt

A handmade baby quilt is something very special that is sure to be cherished for many years. When cutting and making up the quilt, it is important to be extremely accurate so all the pieces fit together perfectly. Use a 5mm (¼in) seam allowance throughout, unless otherwise specified.

YOU WILL NEED ❀ sufficient coordinating fabrics to make 30 squares of 20 x 20cm (8 x 8in)
❀ ruler ❀ pencil ❀ scissors or rotary cutter ❀ cutting mat (optional) ❀ pins
❀ sewing machine ❀ matching thread ❀ iron ❀ 95 x 110cm (37½ x 43¼in) machine-washable
quilt wadding ❀ safety pins ❀ 95 x 110cm (37½ x 43¼in) coordinating backing fabric
❀ needle ❀ contrasting thread ❀ free-motion or darning sewing machine foot
❀ 3.5m (11ft 6in) of 2.5cm (1in) bias binding tape

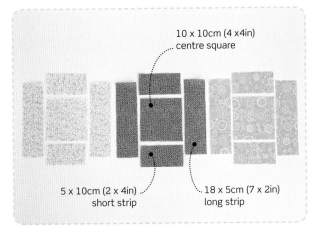

10 x 10cm (4 x4in)
centre square

5 x 10cm (2 x 4in)
short strip

18 x 5cm (7 x 2in)
long strip

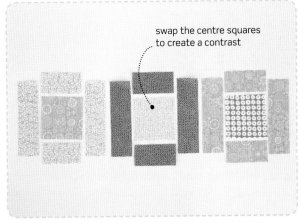

swap the centre squares
to create a contrast

1 **Using scissors or a rotary cutter** and cutting mat, cut each 20 x 20cm (8 x 8in) fabric square into five pieces – one centre square of 10 x 10cm (4 x 4in), two short strips of 5 x 10cm (2 x 4in) and two long strips of 18 x 5cm (7 x 2in).

2 **Swap the centre squares around** so that each finished quilt square will be unique. Lay out all 30 quilt squares in a six-by-five-square pattern, to plan out what the finished quilt will look like.

3 **Pin one short strip** to one side of its centre square, right side to right side. Making sure square and strip are correctly aligned, sew the two together using a straight stitch.

4 **Pin the other short strip** to the opposite side of the square and stitch it in place in the same way. Repeat steps 3 and 4 to attach short strips to all 30 quilt squares.

5 **Lay each quilt square** face down and press open the seam allowances on all 30 pieces.

6 **Pin a long strip** to its quilt square, right side to right side, as shown, and stitch it in place. Repeat with the other long strip along the opposite side of the quilt square. Repeat to make all 30 quilt squares. Press open the seam allowances, as in step 5.

7 **With right side to right side,** pin together two squares from one of the six-square rows. Sew along the edge. Add another square, making sure it is oriented the same way as the first, then another three to give you a strip that is six squares long. Repeat to make a total of five strips of six squares.

8 **Press open the seam allowances** on the back of all the strips. Pin two strips, right sides together, matching the seams as you pin. Stitch the two strips together. Add the remaining three strips. You have now completed the quilt top – a rectangle of six quilt squares by five. Press open all the seam allowances on the back.

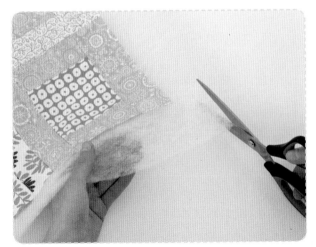

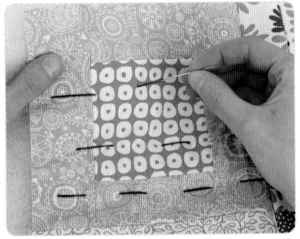

9 **Lay the quilt top right side up** on the wadding. Trim the wadding, leaving approximately 7.5cm (3in) around all four sides of the quilt top. Lay the backing fabric face down, then put the quilt top and the wadding on top. Pin the three layers together evenly with safety pins, making sure the backing fabric is square to the quilt top, then trim the backing fabric to the same size as the wadding.

10 **Using contrasting thread,** tack through all the layers to hold them together. It is very important to make sure all three layers lie flat and are evenly aligned.

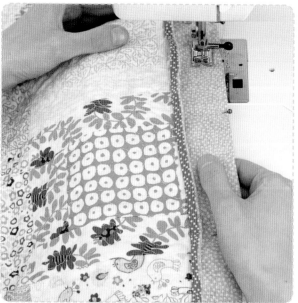

11 **Attach a free-motion foot** or a darning foot to your sewing machine. With the quilt face up, start in one corner and work your way along the edge, stitching all three layers together. You can stitch any pattern you like. As you sew, keep your speed constant, hold the quilt firmly, and move it evenly under the foot. Once you have quilted the entire top, carefully remove the tacking stitches and trim the wadding and backing fabric to the same size as the quilt top.

12 **Starting in the middle of one side** of the quilt, pin the edge of the bias binding along the edge of the quilt, right side to right side, turning over a small hem on the short end of the bias binding first. Sew the quilt and bias binding together leaving a 1cm (½in) seam allowance. When you reach a corner, mitre the bias binding so it lies flat. To mitre the bias binding, remove the quilt from under the presser foot without cutting the threads. Fold the bias binding over and to the right, making a diagonal fold at the corner. Keeping that diagonal fold in place, fold the bias binding back over to the left. Pin the corner, turn the quilt, then pin the binding along the next side and sew it to the quilt as before. Repeat until all four sides have bias binding.

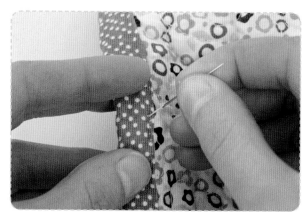

13 **Wrap the bias binding** around the edge of the quilt to the back, folding its raw edge under by 5mm (¼in). Hand-stitch the binding in place to the back of the quilt only, weaving your needle back and forth. Alternatively, you can machine-stitch the binding in place. Pin the folded edge to the quilt first, then machine-stitch carefully from the front so that the stitches sit in the "ditch" created by the seam that attached the binding in step 12.

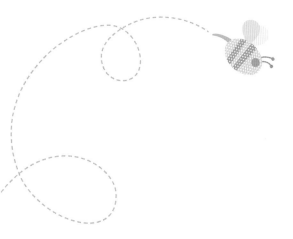

Button bunny

A piece of button art is a fantastic way to brighten up a nursery. You can make your unique work even more special by using the buttons from items of clothing your baby has outgrown.

YOU WILL NEED ❀ craft knife ❀ ruler ❀ thick card ❀ tracing paper ❀ marker pen or pencil ❀ scissors ❀ hot glue gun ❀ glue sticks ❀ selection of buttons, sequins, and beads ❀ 22.5 x 22.5cm (9 x 9in) box frame, or the size of your choice

hot glue gun

1 **Use the craft knife** and ruler to cut the card to fit the box frame. With a marker pen or pencil, trace the bunny template on page 233 onto the tracing paper, then cut it out with scissors. If you prefer, you can make a template using your own design, perhaps one that fits with the theme of baby's nursery.

2 **Centre the template** on the piece of card. Using a pencil, lightly trace around the template to transfer the design onto the card.

3 **Squeeze a small** amount of hot glue onto the back of a button, sequin, or bead, then place the item, glue-side down, inside the traced design. Attach a first layer consisting of larger buttons, sequins, or beads. Work around the edges of the design first, covering the pencilled lines as you go.

4 **Once you have filled** in the design, add a second layer consisting of medium-sized buttons, sequins, or beads. Cover any gaps in the first layer. Continue until most of the gaps are hidden. Finally, fill any remaining gaps with small buttons, sequins, or beads. Once you've finished, fit your piece of art in the box frame.

Flower petals play-mat

see pages 52–55

Decorative nursery hangers

Use these découpaged hangers to show off a few special items from your baby's wardrobe. There are certain to be one or two items, such as the outfit she wore home from the hospital, that you'd like to keep on display. Choose paper and ribbon in colours that complement your nursery.

YOU WILL NEED ✿ white-painted wooden baby hangers ✿ tracing paper ✿ Blu-Tack® ✿ pencil ✿ scissors ✿ low-tack tape ✿ patterned scrapbook paper ✿ soft paintbrush ✿ découpage medium or PVA glue diluted with water to the consistency of thin cream ✿ emery board or fine sandpaper ✿ clear matt or gloss varnish ✿ coordinating ribbon (optional)

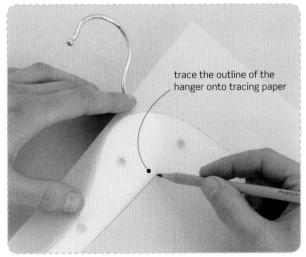

trace the outline of the hanger onto tracing paper

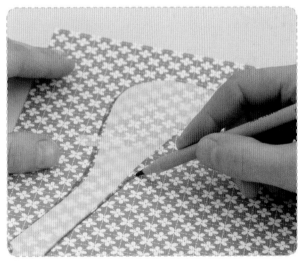

1 **Lay the tracing paper** on the front of the hanger and attach it with dots of Blu-Tack®. Trace the outline of the hanger onto the tracing paper, then cut it out. This will be your template.

2 **Hold the template up** to the hanger to make sure it matches exactly. Make any adjustments necessary. Once you are satisfied with your template, attach it with low-tack tape to the right side of the patterned paper. Trace around it lightly with a pencil.

3 **Remove the template** from the patterned paper, then carefully cut out the paper with scissors.

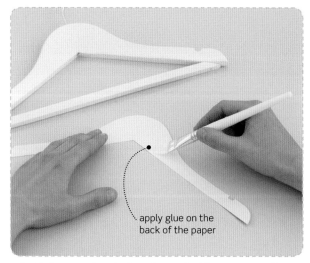

apply glue on the back of the paper

4 **Using a soft paintbrush,** apply découpage medium or diluted PVA glue to the front of the hanger and to the back of the patterned paper. Make sure both are thoroughly covered so there are no unglued areas.

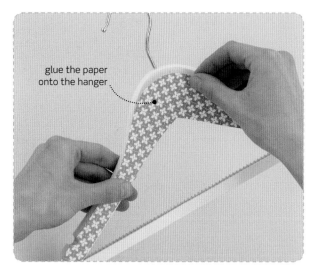

glue the paper onto the hanger

5 **Lay the paper on the front of the hanger,** positioning it carefully. Smooth it out to remove any air bubbles, then coat with a layer of glue to seal the paper. Leave to dry. Repeat for the bottom rail. If desired, repeat steps 1–5 to decorate the back of the hanger.

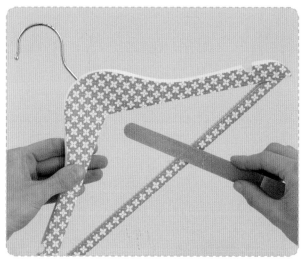

6 **With an emery board or fine sandpaper,** sand the edges of the paper in a downward motion. Continue sanding until the paper becomes one with the hanger. Don't worry if some of the paper and paint are sanded off. This will give the hanger a gently aged look.

7 **Apply another layer of glue** to the paper to seal it again. Pay special attention to the edges of the paper to make sure they don't lift from the hanger.

8 **To protect the paper** and create an attractive finish, apply a few coats of clear varnish. Allow each coat to dry before applying the next. Use matt or gloss varnish, depending on the effect you want to achieve.

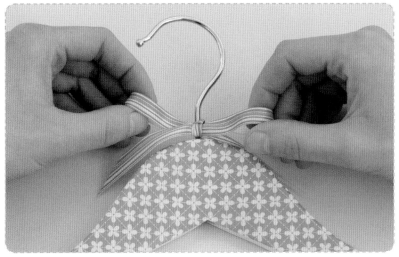

9 **For a pretty finishing touch,** tie a bow made from coordinating ribbon around the top of the hanger. Trim the ends of the ribbon so that they are of even length.

TOP TIP *Hangers that lie flat will be much easier to work with than hangers that curve.*

Counting sheep blanket

Counting the appliqué sheep on this cot blanket is sure to lull your baby off to sleep. You could even try embroidering numbers on them. Follow the layout provided to create our delightful scene or devise a design that's all your own.

YOU WILL NEED ❀ tracing paper ❀ pencil ❀ scissors ❀ pins ❀ scraps of cotton fabrics in whites, creams, beiges, and greens, big enough to fit the template pieces ❀ 30cm (12in) square of white felt or thin wadding to pad the shapes ❀ sewing machine capable of zigzag stitch ❀ white, cream, brown, and green threads ❀ 1 fleece baby blanket with a minimum width of 155cm (61in), in the colour of your choice ❀ needle ❀ contrasting thread for tacking ❀ black embroidery thread ❀ large-eyed needle

1 **With a pencil, trace the templates** provided on page 229 onto your tracing paper. Cut out the templates.

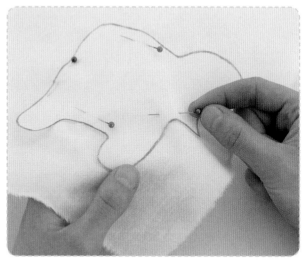

2 **Iron your fabrics** and pin the templates to the wrong side, matching the template to the fabric you have chosen for that piece. In our layout, some sheep face the opposite way from others; for these, flip the template over before pinning it to the fabric.

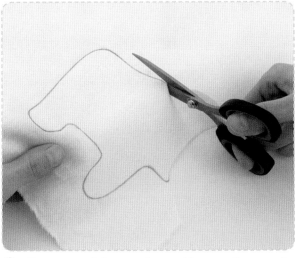

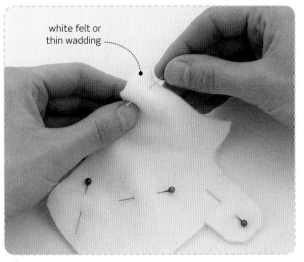

white felt or
thin wadding ......

3 **Trace around the templates** with a pencil to transfer the shape to the fabric. Remove the pins and templates and cut out your fabric pieces.

4 **To pad the shapes,** cut your chosen padding to match the fabric piece, as shown. Pin the padding to the wrong side of the fabric. If you find that too fiddly, cut the padding slightly bigger all round.

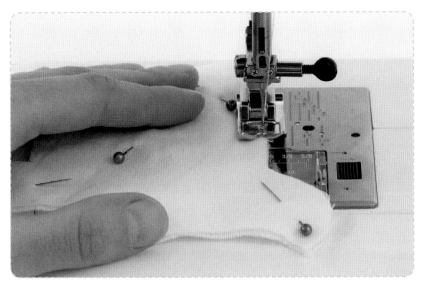

5 **Thread your machine and bobbin** with thread that matches your fabric piece. Using a straight stitch, sew around the fabric and padding, close to the edge, to hold the two layers together. Remove the pins. If you started with slightly bigger padding, trim away the excess.

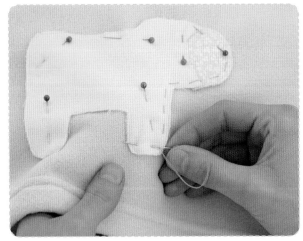

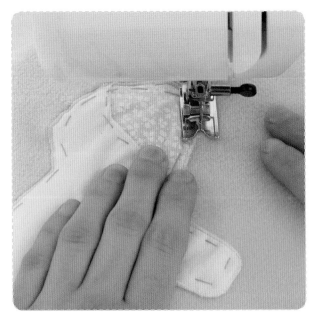

6 **Following the position guide** on page 229, arrange the fabric pieces on the blanket. When you are happy with the arrangement, pin the pieces in place, tucking the edge of the sheep's faces slightly underneath their bodies. Leave the ears until the next step. Using a needle and contrasting thread, tack the pieces securely to the blanket. Remove the pins.

7 **Thread your machine and bobbin** with thread to match your first fabric piece. Set the machine to a wide zigzag stitch with a short 0-1 stitch length, to create a close satin stitch. Neatly stitch around all the pieces that require that colour thread. Tack and zigzag the lamb's ears in place once you have completed the bodies and faces. Thread your machine and bobbin in the next colour and stitch the pieces that require that colour in place. Repeat the process until all the fabric pieces have been attached using the correct colour.

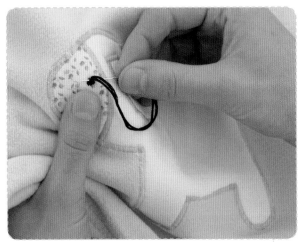

8 **Cut off any loose ends** of thread and remove the tacking stitches. Thread the large-eyed needle with black embroidery thread and embroider a few stitches to create an eye for each sheep.

Fluttery bunting

Bunting is a quick, fun way to brighten up the nursery or a party, such as baby's first birthday party. Just remember to hang the bunting out of reach of babies and children. These instructions will make 3m (9ft 10in) of bunting.

YOU WILL NEED ✿ tracing paper ✿ pencil ✿ scissors ✿ selection of coordinating 17 x 22cm (6¾ x 8½in) fabrics, enough for 26 flags ✿ pins ✿ sewing machine ✿ white thread ✿ pinking shears ✿ 3.1m (10ft 2in) of 2.5cm (1in) bias binding in the colour of your choice ✿ thread to match the bias binding

1 **Trace the flag template** on page 237 onto the tracing paper and cut it out.

2 **Pin the template** to the fabric, making sure that any pattern on the fabric is straight and centred. Cut out the flag. Repeat until you have cut out a total of 26 flags in an assortment of fabrics.

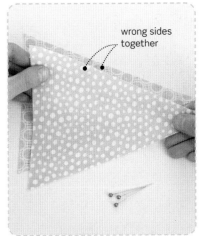

wrong sides together

3 **Put two flags** of different fabrics together so that you have a total of 13 mismatched pairs. Pin each pair together, wrong side to wrong side.

4 **Thread the machine** and bobbin with white thread. Using a straight stitch and leaving a 1cm (½in) seam allowance, stitch together the two long sides of each pair of flags. Repeat for all 13 pairs.

5 **Use pinking shears** to trim the fabric along the stitched sides, close to the edge. Make sure you do not cut through the stitches. Lay the flags out as you would like them to appear in the finished bunting, making sure that flags of the same pattern are not next to each other.

measure 5cm (2in) between each flag ·····

6 **Fold the bias binding in half.** Leaving 7.5cm (3in) of binding free at one end, insert the first flag inside the folded bias binding. Pin it in place, making sure the flag sits evenly against the fold in the binding. Measure 5cm (2in) from the end of the first flag, then pin the next flag in place. Repeat, working your way along the bias binding, until all 13 flags are pinned in place.

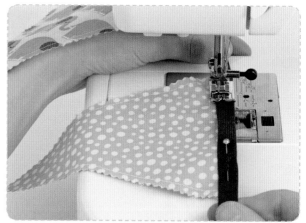

7 **Trim the other end** of the bias binding so 7.5cm (3in) remains free. Thread the machine and bobbin with thread that matches the bias binding. Starting at one end of the binding, carefully straight stitch along the unfolded edge, sewing the flags in place and the folded bias binding together. Remove the pins as you work.

Cosy bath-time penguin pair

Make bath-time lots of fun with this penguin pair. When making the toy, be sure to choose machine-washable toy filling so that it's not a problem if your penguin wants to go for a quick dip in the bath, too.

YOU WILL NEED ❀ tracing paper ❀ pencil ❀ scissors ❀ 1 bath towel, at least 70 x 127cm (27½ x 50in) ❀ 2 white face flannels, at least 30 x 30cm (12 x 12in) each ❀ 1 cream or lemon face flannel, at least 30 x 30cm (12 x 12in) ❀ scraps of black or navy fabric, for eyes ❀ pins ❀ sewing machine capable of zigzag stitch ❀ white thread ❀ bright blue thread ❀ 4m (158in) of 2.5cm (1in) bias binding ❀ thread to match towel ❀ cream or lemon thread ❀ small plate or bowl ❀ tailor's chalk ❀ machine-washable toy filling ❀ needle

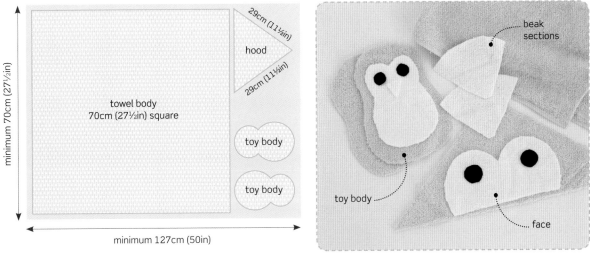

1 **Trace and cut out the templates** from page 232. Lay out the towel and cut the sections to size, as shown in the diagram above.

2 **Cut the penguins' face** and tummy pieces from the white flannels and the beak sections from the cream or lemon flannel. For the eyes, cut two 3cm (1¼in) circles and two 2cm (¾in) circles from the black or navy fabric.

Bath-time penguin wrap

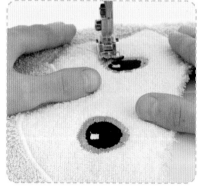

1 **Starting with the** penguin wrap, place the face and the larger pair of eyes on the hood. Pin in place. Using white thread and a straight stitch, machine-stitch around the edges of the face and eyes to secure them in place. Remove all pins.

2 **Set your sewing machine** to a wide zigzag stitch with a short 0-1 stitch length. Sew around the edges of the face in white, then sew a small zigzagged highlight on each eye. Change to bright blue thread and zigzag around each eye.

3 **Cut a piece of bias binding** to fit along the bottom edge. Pin it in place, right sides together. Using matching thread and a straight stitch, machine-stitch the binding in place, about 1cm (½in) from the bottom edge. Remove all pins.

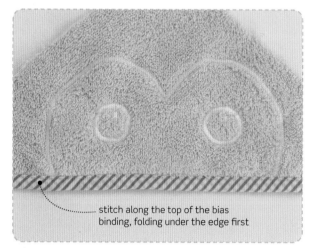

stitch along the top of the bias binding, folding under the edge first

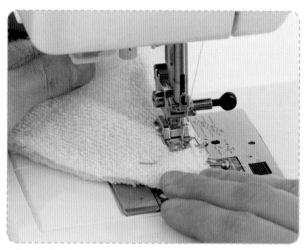

4 **Fold the bias binding** to the back of the hood. Pin in place, making sure the upper edge is folded under. Machine-stitch along the upper edge. Remove all pins.

5 **Pin both beak pieces together.** Using a 1cm (½in) seam allowance and matching thread, sew along the two sides, leaving the top open. Turn right side out.

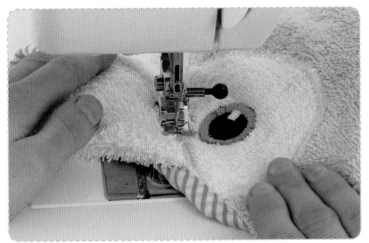

6 **Pin the beak to the face,** on top of the bias binding. Still using the matching thread, straight stitch across the top of the beak to secure it in place. Remove all pins. Then, as in step 2, set your machine to a wide zigzag stitch. Stitch along the top edge of the beak. You may wish to go over these stitches twice if they are not dense enough the first time.

7 **Lay the hood on one corner** of the square towel body and pin it in place along the two outer edges.

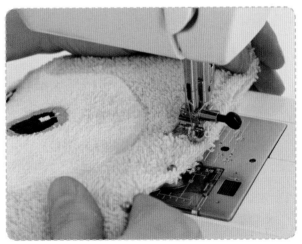

8 **Use a small plate or bowl** and tailor's chalk to mark and round off the four corners of the towel, including the corner with the hood. Make sure you have marked each corner with the same curve. Re-pin the hood to accommodate the curve, then cut along the marks to produce four rounded corners.

9 **Thread your machine and bobbin** with thread to match the towel and set it to a straight stitch. Sew around the outer edges of the hood to attach it. Remove all pins. Finally, repeat steps 3 and 4 to add bias binding to all four edges of the towel.

Bath-time penguin toy

1 **To make the matching penguin toy,** take one toy body section and centre the white face and tummy section on top. Pin in place. Position and pin the smaller pair of eyes and the beak.

2 **Using a straight stitch,** sew close to the edge around the face and tummy section, and around the eyes and beak to secure them in place. Remove the pins.

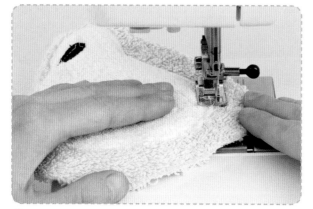

3 **Set your sewing machine** to a wide zigzag stitch with a short 0-1 stitch length. Thread the machine and bobbin with white thread. Zigzag around the face and tummy section and zigzag a small highlight on each eye. Change to the bright blue thread and zigzag around each eye. Finally, change to the lemon or cream thread and zigzag around the beak.

4 **Place the two body sections** right sides together and pin them in place. Thread your machine and bobbin with thread to match the towel and re-set the machine to a straight stitch of normal width and length. Using a 1cm (½in) seam allowance, sew around the edges, leaving an opening of about 5cm (2in) at the bottom.

5 **Clip into the seam allowance** to reduce the bulk and make the curves smoother.

6 **Turn the toy right side out** and stuff firmly with toy filling. Hand-stitch the opening at the bottom of the toy with matching thread.

Heirloom patchwork quilt see pages 22-27

Flower petals play-mat

Make a comfy, colourful mat for baby's playtime. Use bright fabrics, choosing strongly contrasting colours to grab your baby's attention. Remember to wash and dry all the fabrics to pre-shrink them before cutting them out.

YOU WILL NEED ❀ tracing paper ❀ pencil ❀ scissors ❀ pins ❀ 14 scraps of fabric for petals, 20 x 38cm (8 x 15in) minimum per scrap ❀ two pieces of differently patterned main fabrics, 70 x 70cm (27½ x 27½in) each ❀ 33cm (13in) minimum length ruler ❀ tailor's chalk ❀ sewing machine ❀ matching thread ❀ pinking shears ❀ washable toy filling ❀ up to 14 washable squeakers, bells, rattles, pieces of cellophane, or other toy notions (optional) ❀ 2 pieces of wadding, each 70cm (27½in) square ❀ needle

1 **Trace the petal template** on page 233 onto the tracing paper and cut it out. Pin the template to the first piece of fabric and cut around it. Repeat, cutting out two petals from each of the 14 scraps of fabric so that you have a total of 28 petals.

make a mark in the centre of your fabric

2 **Cut out a 64cm (25in)** diameter circle from one of the pieces of main fabric. To do this, mark the centre of the fabric with chalk on the wrong side, then measure and mark a point 32cm (12½in) from the first mark. Continue in a clockwise direction, measuring and marking until you have a circle, then cut it out. Cut a matching circle from the other piece of main fabric.

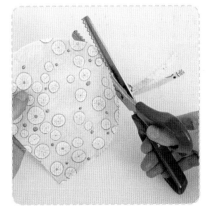

3 **Put two petals** of different fabrics right sides together, then pin each pair. Using a straight machine stitch and matching thread, and leaving a 1cm (½in) seam allowance, sew around the rounded edge of each pair. Leave the straight edge open. Using pinking shears, trim the seam allowance to 5mm (¼in).

4 **Turn each petal right side out and iron.** Lay out one main fabric circle, right side up. Arrange the petals around the circle as you would like them to appear in the finished play-mat, making sure that petals of the same pattern are not next to each other. Lightly stuff each petal with toy filling and, if desired, insert a squeaker or other toy notion.

5 **Arrange the stuffed petals** around the circle with their open, straight edges facing outwards. Pin each petal in place on the circle, making sure the edges of the petals are aligned with the edge of the circle.

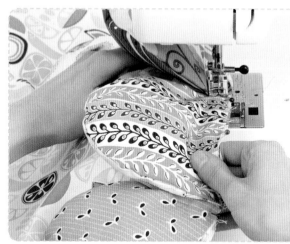

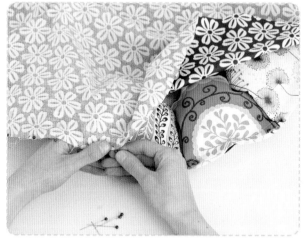

6 **Machine-stitch around the edge of the circle** to stitch the petals in place. Leave a 1cm (½in) seam allowance. Remove all pins. Clip into the seam allowance with scissors to ease the curve around the circle, but do not cut through the stitches.

7 **Lay the second circle of main fabric,** right side down, on top of the petals. Pin all the layers together, sandwiching the petals between the top and bottom circles. Make sure all the edges are aligned.

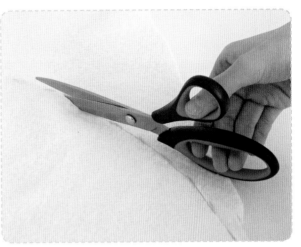

8 **Leaving a 1cm (½in) seam allowance,** sew around the edge to stitch all the layers together. This attaches the petals more securely and should cover the seam that was sewn in step 6. Leave an opening approximately one petal's width in this latest seam.

9 **Turn the mat right side out** through the opening. Measure the diameter of the central circle and cut two pieces of wadding to fit inside, using the technique in step 2. The circle should be approximately 61cm (24in) in diameter.

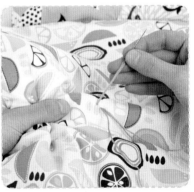

10 **Centre the two pieces** of wadding on top of each other and insert them through the opening in the mat. Make sure the wadding is neither too large and bunched up, nor too small, with gaps between it and the edges of the mat.

11 **Turn under the raw edge** of fabric at the opening and pin it in place on top of the petals. Machine-stitch to close the opening. Measure and lightly mark a circle with chalk 2.5cm (1in) in from the edge of the central circle.

12 **Machine stitch** along this line to secure the wadding in place inside the mat. Measure and mark the centre of the mat and hand-sew a few stitches at this point to secure all the layers together at the centre.

Felt friends mobile

Let this fun-loving gang keep your baby entertained while you're changing him. Remember always to hang your mobile well out of his reach. Mobiles are not toys and you should always supervise your baby when a mobile hangs near.

YOU WILL NEED ✿ tracing paper ✿ pencil or marker pen ✿ scissors ✿ a light, dry twig ✿ paintbrush (optional) ✿ white paint, or paint in the colour of your choice (optional) ✿ pins ✿ scraps of grey, cream, white, tan, red, blue, black, brown, mint, and green felt ✿ small fabric scraps, for animals' clothing ✿ needle ✿ assorted coordinating and contrasting threads ✿ toy filling ✿ hole punch ✿ scrap of white paper ✿ ribbon (optional)

1 **Trace the templates** on pages 230–231 onto the tracing paper and cut them out to make the patterns. Trim the twig and, if desired, paint it in the colour of your choice, then set it aside to dry. Apply as many coats of paint as required.

2 **Pin the patterns** to the felts and fabrics and cut out all of the pieces. Use the photograph opposite and the templates as a guide to which colour to use for which pattern piece.

3 **Embroider an eye** on each elephant piece in contrasting thread, then stitch on the ears in matching thread. Use the instructions on page 59 as your guide for the other animals.

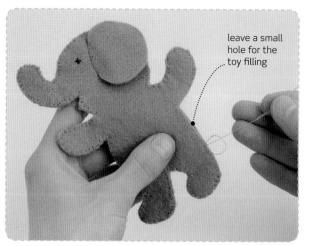

leave a small hole for the toy filling

4 **Make sure to embroider** a mirror image of facial features and body parts on the second animal piece so that when you stitch the two together you have the correct features on both pieces.

5 **Using blanket stitch** (see p.224), sew together the two halves of the body, leaving a small hole through which you can stuff it.

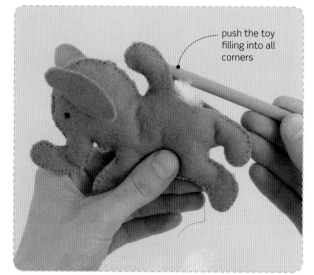

push the toy filling into all corners

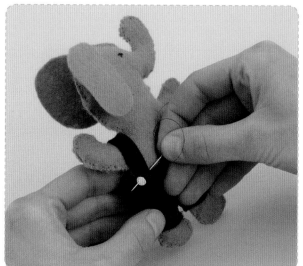

6 **Lightly stuff the animal** with the toy filling. Use the end of a pencil to work the filling into all the corners that are otherwise difficult to stuff. When you have finished stuffing the animal, use blanket stitch to sew up the hole.

7 **Join the elephant's trousers** at the sides and the crotch. Slip the trousers on his body. Attach the straps at the front and back and finish by sewing on a white circle of hole-punched paper for the buttons. Use the instructions opposite as a guide for the other animals.

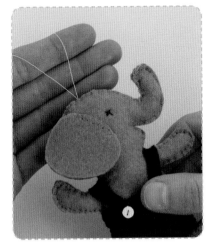

8 **Use white thread** and a needle to create a loop at the top of each animal's head for it to hang from. Vary the length of the loops so the animals will all hang at different heights.

9 **Once the twig is dry, arrange the animals on it.** Their weight should be evenly distributed so the twig hangs level. To secure them in place, loop them over the twig then pass each animal through its own loop. Use a piece of thread or ribbon to hang the mobile safely out of baby's reach.

STITCHING THE ANIMALS

Fox: Embroider the shirt pattern. Sew the white tail and face sections to the body, then embroider the face. Sew together the two halves of the body and stuff. Sew the front seam of the shirt, then place it around the front of the body and sew the back seam closed. Stitch together and stuff the arms, then place one on either side of the body and attach at the top.

Giraffe: Sew on the spots, then embroider the eyes and stitch both halves of the body together. Sew the back seam of the dress, then hem the bottom and top edges, leaving long thread tails on the top. Slip the dress over the body and pull the thread tails to gather it around the body, then tack it in place. Stitch together and stuff both arms, then attach one arm to either side of the body, over the dress. Sew a horn to either side of the head, then sew an ear over each horn.

Squirrel: Embroider an eye on either side of the head, then stitch and stuff the body. Sew the front seam of the shirt, then place it around the front of the body and sew the back seam closed. Stitch together and stuff both arms, then sew one arm on either side of the body. Finally, attach an ear to either side of the head.

Cat: Stitch on the stripes and nose, then embroider the face. Stitch the body together with a straight stitch. Sew the front seam of the trousers and place them along the body, then sew the crotch and the back seams, leaving a hole for the tail.

Donkey: Sew on the nose sections and embroider the eyes. Sew the body together with a straight stitch, sandwiching the mane in place between both halves. Attach the ears. Sew the back seam of the skirt, then hem the bottom and top edges, leaving long thread tails on the top. Slip the skirt over the body and pull the thread tails to gather it around the body, then tack it in place. Stitch the nose piece of the halter at the bottom, then slip it around the nose. Stitch one side of the rein in place, adding a hole-punched circle of paper as a button, then wrap the rein around to the other side and stitch it in place in the same way.

Fairy tale house doorstop

Practical and cute, this whimsical little house can be used as a doorstop or a bookend. Copy the design exactly, using the templates provided at the back of the book, or choose your own colours and embroidery and felt details.

YOU WILL NEED ❀ an empty, clean juice carton, approximately 17 x 10 x 7cm (6¾ x 4 x 2¾ in) ❀ scissors ❀ pencil or marker pen ❀ ruler ❀ approximately 500g (17½oz) dried lentils ❀ toy filling ❀ masking tape ❀ paper ❀ light blue, dark purple, light purple, an assortment of green, dark brown, light brown, tan, grey, pink, red, orange, and yellow felts ❀ tracing paper ❀ embroidery needle ❀ embroidery threads to match the felts, plus white ❀ pins

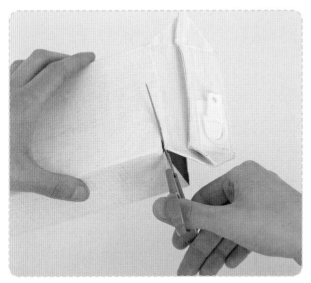

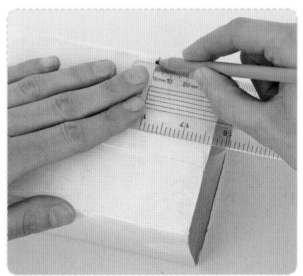

1 **Cut the top from the old juice** carton using scissors. Discard the top of the carton.

2 **With the cut edge as the top,** measure and mark 4cm (1½in) from each of the four corners. Cut along each corner of the carton to the marked points to create four flaps.

3 **Fold the longer flaps** inwards so they meet at the centre of the carton. Use a pencil to mark the angle of the longer flaps where they abut the short flaps. This creates the roof line.

4 **Cut along the angled** lines to make the roof gables.

5 **Fill the container** with dried lentils to the crease line of the two longer flaps. This gives the doorstop its weight.

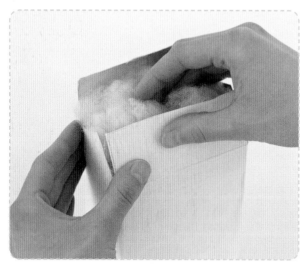

6 **Add toy filling to the very top,** to fill the roof void, then fold the longer flaps to meet the gables and secure in place with masking tape. Make sure to cover every join so that no lentils can escape.

7 **Stand each face of the house** in turn on a piece of paper and draw around each one, leaving a gap between the outlines. These will be your templates for cutting the felt that covers the house.

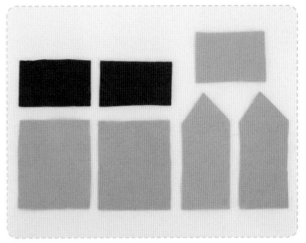

8 **Add 5mm (¼in) around each outline** for the seam allowances. Cut each template out, including the seam allowances.

9 **Pin the templates to the** correct pieces of felt and accurately cut the felt out. You should have one house front, one back, two sides, and one base in light blue felt and two roof pieces in dark purple felt.

10 **Trace the templates on pages 246–247** onto the tracing paper and cut out the pieces to make the patterns for the house details. Pin the patterns to the correct pieces of felt and cut them out. In addition, cut a 30 x 1cm (12 x ½in) strip each of red, orange, yellow, green, blue, and purple felt, and one 30 x 3.5cm (12 x 1⅜in) strip of dark purple felt, as shown.

11 **Using the stitch guides** on the templates and the appropriate colours, embroider the details onto the various felt shapes.

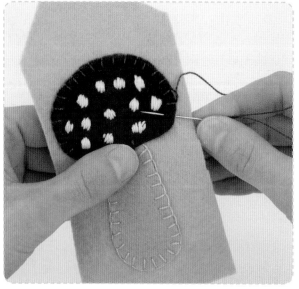

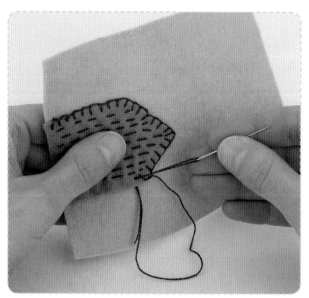

12 **Sew the felt shapes** to the sides, front, back, and roof of the house using the templates and embroidery stitches on pages 224–225 as a reference.

13 **Continue sewing on** all the small felt shapes, then add the embroidered flowers around the door.

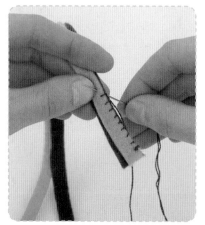

14 **To make the rainbow** handle, blanket stitch the red and orange strips of felt together, along their long side.

15 **Turn the joined strips** over and stretch them gently so they lie flat, then attach the yellow strip. Repeat steps 14 and 15, attaching the green, blue, and purple strips.

16 **Sew the completed** rainbow to the wider strip of dark purple felt, again using blanket stitch. Sew completely around all four edges using blanket stitch.

17 **Join one side** of the house to the front using blanket stitch. Continue joining all the other pieces together, including the roof pieces, until all but the base of the house is attached.

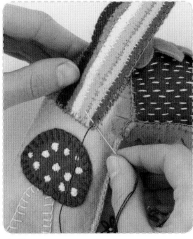

18 **Attach the scallop** details to the roof ridge, gables, and bottom edges, then securely sew the rainbow handle to the top of each side of the house.

19 **Cover each end of** the handle with a grey cloud, pinning the cloud in place first, then attaching it with blanket stitch.

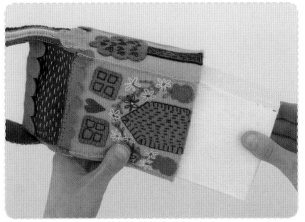

20 **Slip the prepared weighted** juice carton into the completed felt house shape.

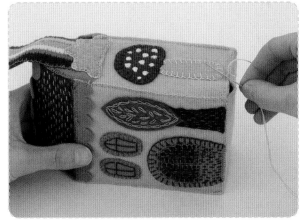

21 **Attach the felt base** with blanket stitch to complete the house.

Starry night swaddle blanket

Personalizing a bought item, such as a baby blanket, can make it that extra bit special. Rubber stamps are simple to make and once you've made one, you can use it over and over again. If you prefer, you can adapt the technique shown below to make your own unique stamp design.

YOU WILL NEED ✿ pencil ✿ ruler ✿ tracing paper ✿ 8 x 8cm (3 x 3in) rubber stamp sheet ✿ masking tape ✿ bone folder (optional) ✿ small v-shaped rubber- or lino-cutting gouge ✿ large u-shaped rubber- or lino-cutting gouge ✿ small foam paint roller ✿ fabric paint ✿ plain swaddle or cot blanket ✿ newspaper ✿ iron (optional)

1 **Using a pencil and ruler,** trace the star template on page 241 onto the tracing paper.

pencil over the outline

2 **Lay the tracing paper** on the rubber stamp sheet with the pencilled lines face down. Secure the tracing paper with masking tape. Pencil over the lines to transfer the design to the rubber stamp sheet. Alternatively, transfer the design by rubbing it with the bone folder or with your finger.

use the small, v-shaped gouge for the outline

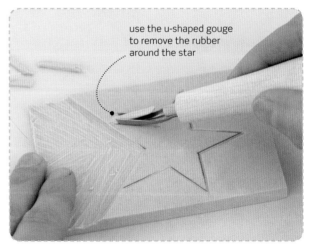

use the u-shaped gouge to remove the rubber around the star

3 **Remove the tracing paper** from the rubber stamp sheet then use the small v-shaped gouge to gouge out the outline of the star. For safety and accuracy, keep the gouge still and move the rubber sheet.

4 **Once you have gouged the outline,** use the large u-shaped gouge to cut away the rubber sheet around the star, leaving the star intact. You now have your star-shaped rubber stamp.

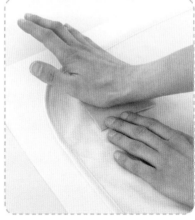

5 **Using the foam paint roller,** apply fabric paint to the stamp, making sure the paint is evenly distributed.

6 **Lay the blanket** right side up on a flat surface, on top of newspaper or another protective material to protect the surface below. Place the stamp on top of the blanket and press it down, applying firm, even pressure.

7 **Carefully remove** the stamp, then repeat steps 5 and 6, positioning each star according to your layout. Reapply paint to the stamp after each print. Set the paint according to the manufacturer's instructions, usually by ironing.

TOP TIP Wash and dry the stencilled fabric following the manufacturer's instructions.

Simple striped frame

Create a bespoke picture frame for your baby's nursery in a simple geometric design. This easy technique uses nothing more than paint and masking tape.

YOU WILL NEED ✿ wooden picture frame in a size of your choice ✿ masking tape ✿ fine-grit sandpaper ✿ acrylic paint in main and second colour ✿ paintbrush ✿ craft knife ✿ cutting mat ✿ ruler ✿ ribbon (optional)

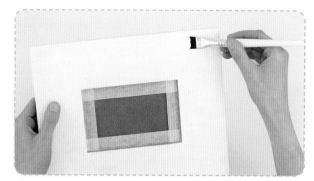

1 **Remove the back** of the frame and the glass or protect the glass from paint with masking tape. Lightly sand the front of the frame to help the paint adhere, then paint the frame in the colour of your choice. Apply two or three coats, letting the paint dry between coats.

2 **Use masking tape to create a stencil** for the second paint colour. Cut the masking tape with a craft knife to the widths and lengths you need to fit your particular frame. Work out the design on the cutting mat, using the ruler guides to help you.

3 **With the masking tape** cut to the required sizes, peel the tape off of the cutting mat and transfer the design to the frame. Make sure the edges of the tape are well stuck down so paint cannot seep underneath.

4 **Paint over the stencil** with the second paint colour. The paint will cover the areas that aren't masked off. When the paint is dry, apply another coat to ensure the paint is even and opaque and that none of the main paint colour shows through.

5 **When the paint is completely dry,** remove the masking tape to reveal your design. Place your picture in the frame and, if you like, hang the picture using some coordinating ribbon.

Fluttery bunting see pages 40–43

Cuddly owl cushion

This little owl cushion will liven up any space. The button eyes mean the cushion cannot be used as a toy, but if you'd like it to be a toy, simply embroider the eyes and omit the buttons.

YOU WILL NEED ✿ pencil or marker pen ✿ tissue or tracing paper ✿ scissors ✿ pins ✿ 35 x 60cm (13¾ x 23½in) body fabric ✿ 20 x 20cm (8 x 8in) patterned wing fabric ✿ 5 x 10cm (2 x 4in) grey eye fabric ✿ 11 x 21cm (4½ x 8¼in) white mask fabric ✿ 8 x 6cm (3 x 2½in) patterned nose fabric ✿ iron ✿ tailor's chalk ✿ ruler ✿ 1m (39½in) rick-rack ✿ sewing machine capable of zigzag stitch ✿ threads to match the main, eye, mask, nose, and wing fabrics ✿ two 2cm (¾in) buttons ✿ thread to match the buttons ✿ needle ✿ toy filling

1 **Enlarge the templates** on page 239 to the specified size, then trace them onto tracing or tissue paper and cut them out to make the pattern pieces.

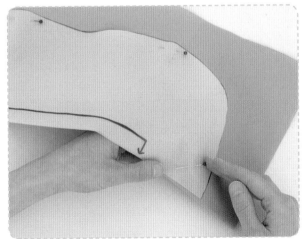

2 **Pin the pattern pieces** to the correct fabrics, making sure to place any fold marks, indicated on the templates with arrows, along a fold in the fabric. Cut around the pattern pieces, unpin them from the fabrics, and unfold the fabrics. Iron the fabric pieces.

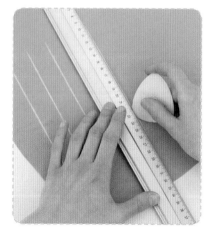

3 **Use tailor's chalk** and a ruler to draw six parallel lines on the owl's belly, between the wings. Space the lines 2.5cm (1in) apart.

4 **Cut lengths of rick-rack** to sit on top of each chalked line and slightly underneath the edge of each wing. Pin the rick-rack in place, making sure it is straight.

5 **Thread your machine** with thread to match the rick-rack and, with a straight stitch, sew down the centre of each length of rick-rack to secure it in place. Remove the pins as you work.

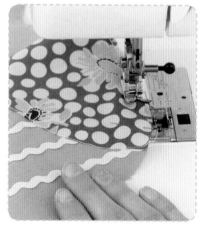

6 **Pin the wings** in place on either side of the belly and overlapping the ends of the rick-rack. Sew completely around the edges of each wing with a straight stitch.

7 **With both a top** and bottom thread in your machine in a complementary colour and using a wide zigzag stitch with a short 0–1 stitch length, zigzag a decorative edge along the inner edge of each wing.

8 **Centre and pin the eyes** to the white mask. Sew around the edges of the eyes with a straight stitch. Thread the machine with grey thread and set it to a wide zigzag stitch with a short stitch length. Zigzag around both eyes.

9 **Pin the mask with its eyes** to the front of the owl's head. Using white thread, straight-stitch then zigzag around the edge, as in step 8. Add the nose and attach in the same way using coordinating thread.

10 **Sew a button eye** to the centre of each fabric eye with a needle and matching thread. Make sure the buttons are securely attached so that they cannot be pulled off and present a choking hazard.

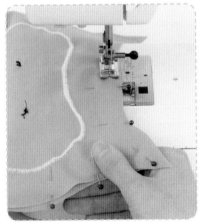

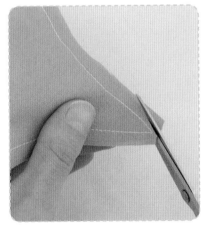

11 **Pin the front and back** of the owl with right sides together. Using matching thread and a straight stitch, sew around the edges, leaving a 1cm (½in) seam allowance. Leave a hole of approximately 7.5cm (3in) at the bottom of the owl.

12 **Trim the seam** allowance around the owl's ears to approximately 5mm (¼in). Clip into the seam allowance around all the corners and curves to reduce the bulk and make the curves smoother.

13 **Turn the owl** right side out through the hole in the bottom and iron. Stuff the cushion with toy filling, then hand-sew the hole closed, weaving your needle back and forth.

Folding changing mat

With this practical changing mat to hand, you'll always have somewhere clean to change your baby, even when you're on the go. PVC makes a good choice for the backing fabric. When not in use, the mat folds in thirds, then in half, and can then be secured with a bow at the side.

YOU WILL NEED ❀ 70 x 55cm (27½ x 22in) each of two different fabrics, such as one cotton and one PVC fabric ❀ cutting mat (optional) ❀ rotary cutter or scissors ❀ 65cm (25½in) cotton tape, 1cm (½in) wide ❀ tailor's chalk ❀ pins ❀ tissue paper (if using PVC fabric) ❀ matching thread ❀ sewing machine ❀ iron ❀ piece of stiff card ❀ 65 x 50cm (25½ x 20in) wadding ❀ straight edge ❀ needle

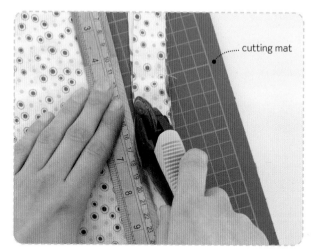

cutting mat

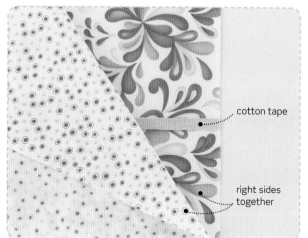

cotton tape

right sides together

1 **Using the cutting mat** and rotary cutter, if used, or your scissors, cut the two fabrics into 62 x 47cm (24½ x 18½in) rectangles. Make sure the fabric is lying completely flat and straight before you cut it. Also cut two pieces of cotton tape, each 30cm (12in) long.

2 **Measure 30cm (12in) down** the long side of one fabric rectangle. Mark that point with chalk on the right side of the fabric. Lay the end of one piece of tape at the marked point, as shown. Repeat on the opposite side, making sure both tapes are level with one another. Place the second piece of fabric on top, right side down.

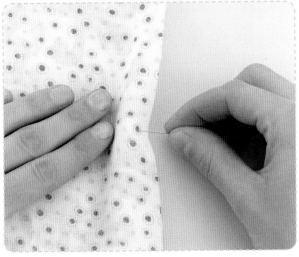

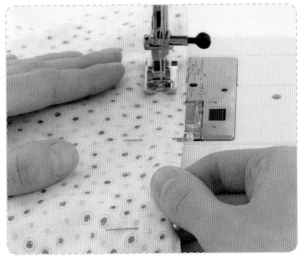

3 **Pin both pieces of fabric** together around all four sides of the rectangle, making sure the tape is pinned in the correct place on both sides. The tape will be sandwiched between the two fabrics.

4 **Using a straight stitch** and matching thread, sew around all four sides. Leave an opening approximately 13cm (5¼in) wide in the short bottom edge. Use tissue paper over the PVC to help it glide through the machine.

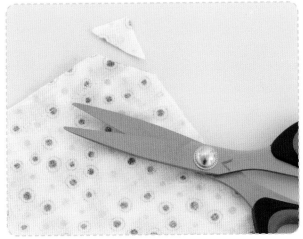

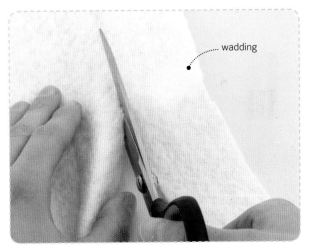

wadding

5 **Snip diagonally across** the four corners to remove the excess fabric, taking care not to cut through the stitches. Turn the changing mat right side out and iron it flat. Use a piece of stiff card pushed into the corners to square them up while ironing.

6 **Measure your changing mat,** then use tailor's chalk and a straight edge to measure and mark a piece of wadding to the same dimensions. Cut it out and insert it through the opening in the mat. Make sure the wadding is neither too large and bunched up nor too small, with gaps between it and the edges of the mat.

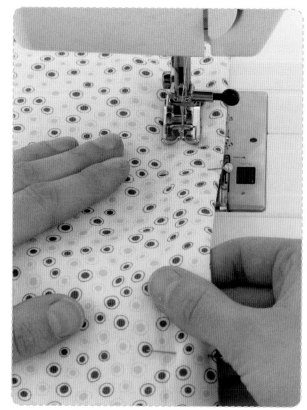

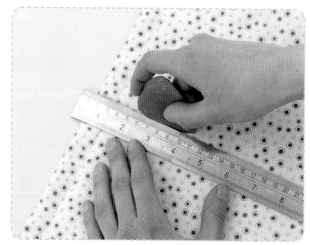

8 **Using the chalk and straight edge,** measure and mark the mat 19cm (7½in) from the top and bottom edges. Join the marks to make two lines along these points. Sew along the lines, stopping when you reach the stitching made in step 7.

7 **When you are happy** with the way the wadding fits inside the changing mat, pin the sides through all three layers. Sew with a straight stitch along all four sides, about 2.5cm (1in) from the edge. This row of stitches will secure the wadding inside the changing mat and prevent it from moving around or bunching up when the mat is washed.

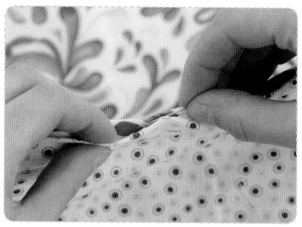

9 **Finish by sewing up** the opening in the bottom edge of the mat by hand. For an invisible finish, weave the needle back and forth between the two layers of fabric at the opening, catching it on alternate sides. Prevent the ends of the tape unravelling by folding them over twice and hand-stitching a straight seam through all three layers.

Hanging cot organizer

Keep essential nursery items to hand with this hanging organizer.
Once your baby is old enough to reach and grab things from it, make sure
you don't leave anything in it that would be unsafe for baby to have.

YOU WILL NEED ❀ 105 x 114cm (41½ x 45in) backing fabric ❀ 55 x 65cm (21½ x 25½in) wadding
❀ 90 x 93cm (35½ x 36½in) pocket fabric ❀ ruler ❀ scissors ❀ iron ❀ pins
❀ tailor's chalk in two colours ❀ sewing machine capable of zigzag stitch ❀ matching thread
❀ pencil ❀ 60cm (23½in) length of 1.5cm (⅝in) diameter wooden dowel

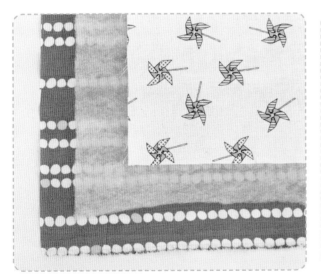

1 **Cut out one rectangle** of backing fabric, 114 x 65cm
(45 x 25½in); two rectangles of pocket fabric, both
45 x 93cm (17¾ x 36½in); and four rectangles of
backing fabric, 40 x 10cm (15¾ x 4in), for the ties.
Iron all the fabrics.

2 **With the short edge** of the backing fabric at the top,
measure and mark a line halfway down the long edge
to divide the fabric into two 57 x 65cm (22½ x 25½in)
sections. The bottom section will be the back of the
organizer and the top section the front. Pin the 55 x
65cm (21½ x 25½in) wadding to the wrong side of the
front, starting 5cm (2in) from the top edge: this is
where the wooden dowel will go.

POCKET FOLD AND STITCH MARK GUIDES

✿ **Lower pocket strip** Make fold marks by marking 23cm (9in), 14cm (5½in), 19cm (7½in), 14cm (5½in), and 23cm (9in) apart, starting from one edge. Mark the centre of the two 14cm (5½in) sections for the stitch marks.

✿ **Upper pocket strip** Repeat using the second strip, but make fold marks spaced 13cm (5¼in) then 7cm (2¾in) alternating to the end of the strip. Mark the centre of each 7cm (2¾in) section for the stitch marks.

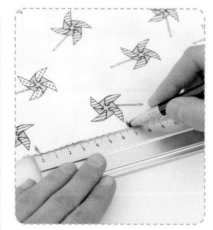

3 **Fold the pocket rectangles** in half to make two 22.5 x 93cm (8¾ x 36½in) strips. Zigzag the long, raw edges, then follow the instructions on page 227 to make the fold and stitch marks using the measurements, left.

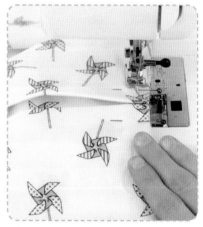

4 **Still following the instructions** on page 227, fold and pin the strips along the fold marks so the folds meet at the centre stitch marks. Iron the folds, then stitch along the bottom edge of each strip to hold the folds in place.

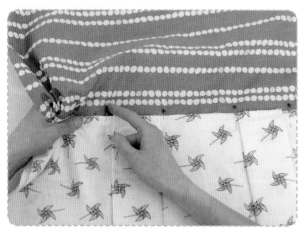

5 **Place the lower pocket strip** right side down on the backing fabric along the line marked in step 2. Position it so its folded edge faces towards the bottom back section and its raw, pleated edge is 5cm (2in) above the marked line. Pin the raw edge in place through the backing fabric and wadding, then stitch in place, leaving a 1cm (½in) seam allowance.

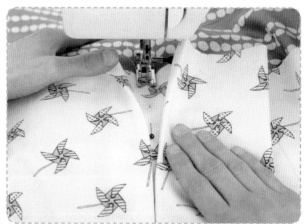

6 **Turn the pocket strip** so it is right side up. Align and pin its edges with the edges of the backing fabric and of the wadding. Pin the strip through the backing fabric and wadding along the centre marks made in step 3. Stitch along the centre marks to form the pleats, then stitch the pinned edges.

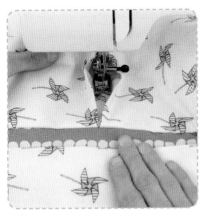

7 **Repeat steps 5 and 6 to** make the upper pocket strip, but position its raw, pleated edge 27.5cm (10¾in) above the line marked in step 2. This will ensure a 2cm (¾in) gap between the upper and lower row of pockets when the pockets are both in position.

8 **Make the ties** by folding and pinning each tie strip, right side to right side, to make four 5 x 40cm (2 x 15¾in) ties. Sew along one end of each and along its long edge, leaving a 1cm (½in) seam allowance. Turn each tie right side out by pushing the sewn end with a blunt pencil.

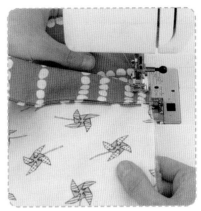

9 **Iron the ties,** then place the raw edges of two of the ties on top of each other, at either side of the upper row of pockets. Align all the raw edges, then stitch them firmly in place.

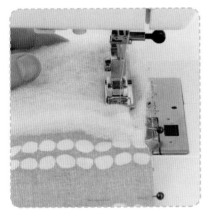

10 **Fold the backing fabric** right side to right side along the line marked in step 2, covering the pockets. Align and pin the raw edges together, then stitch along the sides, through all the layers, leaving the top edge unsewn. Turn the organizer right side out and iron.

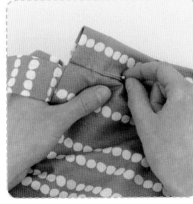

11 **Make the channel** for the wooden dowel by turning the top edge of the backing fabric under 1cm (½in). Iron, then turn it under again by 3cm (1¼in). Pin in place then stitch along the folded and pinned edge.

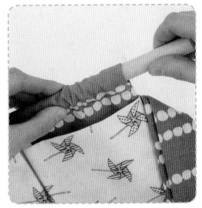

12 **Insert the dowel** into the channel, then machine-stitch the ends of the channel closed.

Anti-slam door wrap

This practical door wrap can be made in under an hour and is a handy way to stop doors banging closed while baby is napping. Choose fun, playful fabrics that complement your room.

YOU WILL NEED ❀ 18 x 18cm (7 x 7in) main fabric ❀ 15 x 30.5cm (6 x 12in) strap fabric ❀ tailor's chalk ❀ ruler ❀ scissors ❀ pins ❀ sewing machine ❀ matching thread ❀ safety pin ❀ 36cm (14in) of 5mm (¼in) elastic ❀ toy filling ❀ needle

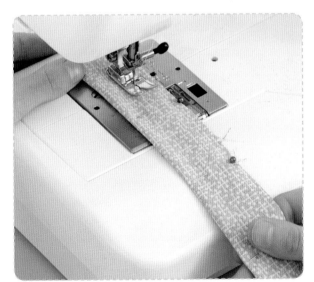

1 **Using tailor's chalk** and a ruler, measure and mark the main fabric so you have two 18 x 9cm (7 x 3½in) rectangles, then measure and mark the strap fabric, so you have two 7.5 x 30.5cm (3 x 12in) rectangles. Cut the fabric rectangles out.

2 **Fold the strap fabric** in half lengthways, right sides together. Pin along the edge, making sure the edges are properly aligned. Using a straight stitch and matching thread, sew along the pinned edge, leaving a 1cm (½in) seam allowance. Remove the pins as you work. Trim the seam allowance to 5mm (¼in). Repeat for the other strap.

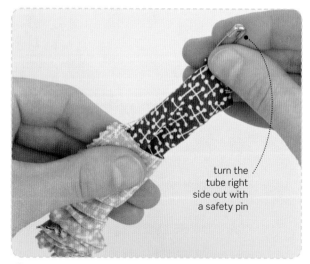

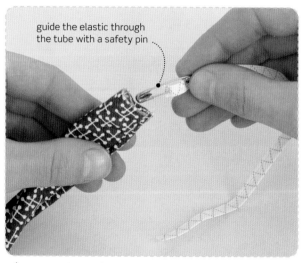

guide the elastic through
the tube with a safety pin

turn the
tube right
side out with
a safety pin

3 **Attach a safety pin** to one end of the strap and push it through the strap. When the safety pin emerges at the other end, pull on it to turn the strap through to the right side (see p.226). Remove the safety pin.

4 **Cut a piece of elastic** 18cm (7in) long. Attach a safety pin to one end and push it through the strap until the unpinned edge of the elastic lines up with the end of the strap.

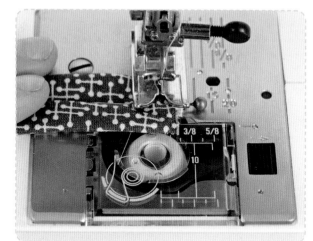

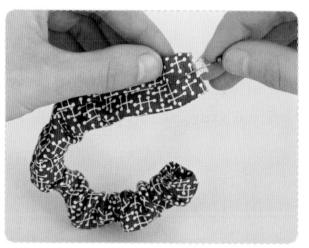

5 **Pin the end of the elastic** so it is centred on the end of the strap, then machine-stitch it in place, leaving a 5mm (¼in) seam allowance.

6 **Work the safety pin** with its elastic through the strap. As you go, the strap will gather along the elastic. When the safety pin emerges at the other end, pin this end of the elastic in place so it is lined up with, and centred on, the edge of the strap. Remove the safety pin and sew the elastic in place as in step 5. Repeat steps 3–6 for the other strap.

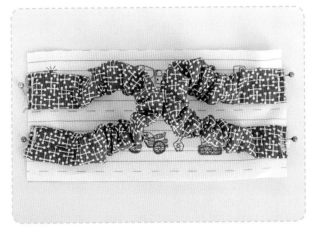

7 **Lay one of the main fabric rectangles** right side up and pin the two straps in place on top of it, as shown. Make sure that the straps are level with one another on either side and that their ends are the same width apart on either side.

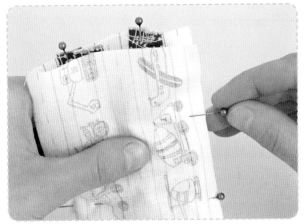

8 **Lay the other main fabric rectangle** right side down on top, making sure that the pattern of the fabric on both rectangles is the same way up. Pin the two rectangles together, matching all four edges as you pin. Pin the sandwiched ends of the straps securely so they cannot move out of place.

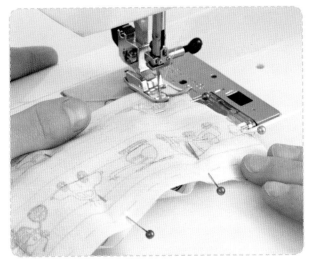

9 **Leaving a 1cm (½in) seam allowance,** sew around all four edges, removing the pins as you sew. Leave a 4cm (1½in) hole in the bottom edge. Forward- and reverse-stitch over the ends of the straps several times to make sure the straps are securely sewn in place and cannot be pulled out.

10 **Turn the door wrap** right side out through the hole in the bottom edge. Stuff it with toy filling, then sew the hole closed using a needle and matching thread.

Water-resistant handy bag

A water-resistant bag is handy for storing damp items after any little accidents or for bringing home dirty cloth nappies. PUL fabric is water-resistant on one side and fabric on the other, so it's perfect for a project such as this one.

YOU WILL NEED ✿ 40 x 64cm (16 x 25¼in) PUL fabric ✿ tailor's chalk ✿ tape measure ✿ scissors ✿ pins ✿ coordinating zip, at least 33cm (13in) long ✿ matching polyester thread ✿ sewing machine ✿ tissue paper or a Teflon® foot for the sewing machine ✿ iron

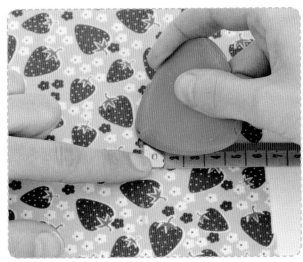

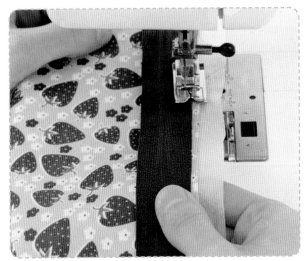

1 **Cut two rectangles** from the PUL fabric, one measuring 30 x 64cm (12 x 25¼in) for the bag and one measuring 6 x 40cm (2½ x 15¾in) for the handle.

2 **Align and pin the zip** to one of the 30cm (12in) edges of the bag fabric, right side to right side. Stitch together leaving a 5mm (¼in) seam allowance. A Teflon® machine foot makes this easier, otherwise place tissue paper against the laminated side of the fabric and tear it away after stitching.

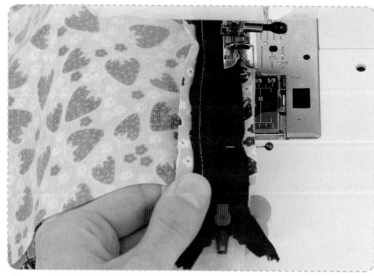

3 **Fold the fabric to align** its other 30cm (12in) edge with the opposite side of the zip, right side to right side. Pin and sew along the edge, leaving a 5mm (¼in) seam allowance and again using tissue paper. Iron on a low temperature, then turn the bag right side out.

4 **Fold the handle lengthways,** right side to right side. Machine with a 1cm (½in) seam allowance. Turn through using a safety pin (see p.226). Iron.

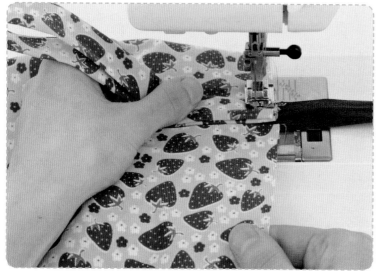

5 **Fold the handle in half** and align the ends with the edge of the bag at the bottom end of the zip. Stitch in place 1cm (½in) from the edge, only sewing through one layer of the bag.

6 **Turn the bag wrong side out** so the back of the zip is facing you. Fold the top edge over so that the zip sits 5.5cm (2¼in) from the top and pin as shown. Open up the zip halfway.

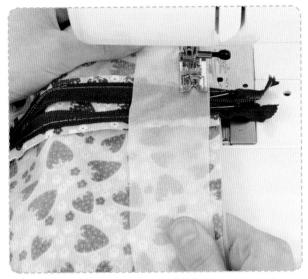

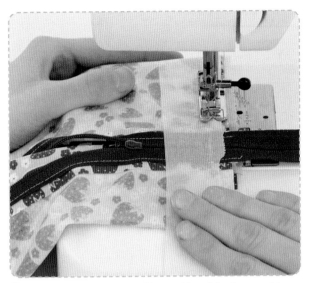

7 **Lay tissue paper above and below** the bag and stitch down one long side of the bag through the open end of the zip, as shown, leaving a 1cm (½in) seam allowance. Remove the pins and tissue paper.

8 **Repeat on the second long side** of the bag, making sure the handle is sandwiched inside and the top edge is folded over level with the opposite side so the zip sits evenly.

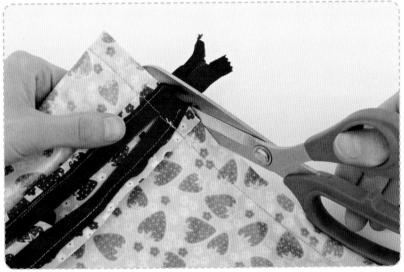

9 **Cut off the excess zip at each end,** then turn the bag to the right side, through the open zip. Iron on a low temperature or according to the manufacturer's instructions.

SIZE
The final bag measures 28 x 31.5cm (11 x 12¼in)

Toys

Lovable whale

This squishy, cuddly, stuffed whale will brighten any day and is sure to become baby's firm favourite. With only three simple seams, our whale is very quick to sew. Why not make an entire family of whales in different, bright fabrics?

YOU WILL NEED ❀ tracing paper ❀ marker pen ❀ scissors ❀ 51 x 35.5cm (20 x 14in) fabric ❀ pins ❀ sewing machine ❀ matching thread ❀ large-eyed needle ❀ black embroidery thread ❀ small embroidery hoop (optional) ❀ toy filling ❀ pencil ❀ needle

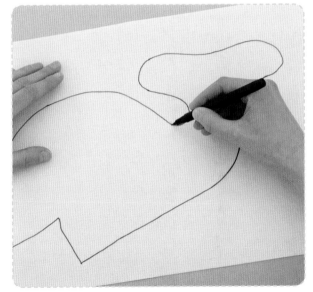

1 **Trace the template** on page 237 onto the tracing paper and cut it out to make the pattern piece.

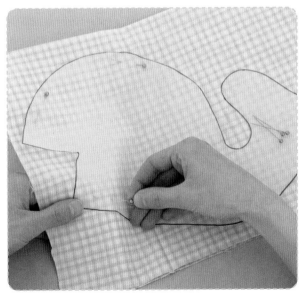

2 **With the fabric folded in half,** wrong side to wrong side, lay the pattern piece on top and pin it in place through both layers. Cut the fabric out. You will then have the front and back of the whale.

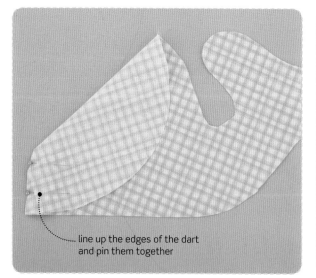

line up the edges of the dart
and pin them together

3 **Pin the edges of the dart together** on the back of
the whale, with right side to right side. Make sure the
slightly curved edges of the dart are correctly aligned.

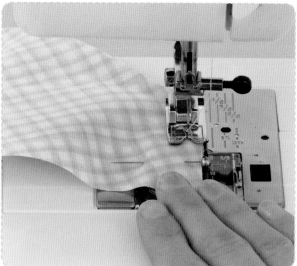

4 **Leaving a 5mm (¼in) seam** allowance, sew along
the pinned edges of the dart. Repeat steps 3 and 4
for the front of the whale.

5 **Using the large-eyed needle** and black embroidery
thread, embroider eyes on the front and back of the
whale. Use an embroidery hoop if you wish. Make
sure the eyes line up on both pieces.

start by matching
and pinning the
two darts

6 **Pin the front and back** of the whale together, right
side to right side. Start by matching the darts, tucking
one inside the other, then work around the edges,
making sure the front and back match up perfectly.

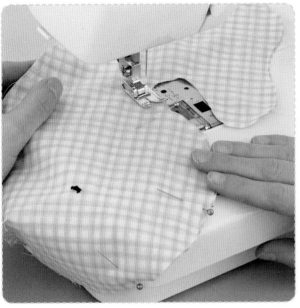

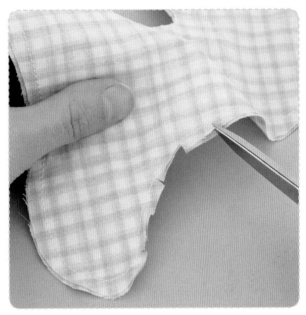

7 **Leaving a 1cm (½in) seam** allowance and starting on the whale's belly, sew around the tail, over the back, and around the head. Finish on the belly, leaving a hole of approximately 6.5cm (2½in).

8 **Clip into the seam allowance** around all the corners and curves to reduce the bulk and make the curves smoother. On the tighter curves, clip more closely.

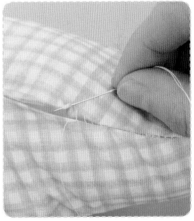

9 **Turn the whale** right side out, through the hole in the belly that you left in step 7.

10 **Firmly stuff the whale** with toy filling, using the blunt end of a pencil to push the filling into the tail.

11 **Sew the hole** in the belly closed, weaving your needle back and forth to catch the opposite edges of the fabric.

Pretty papered building blocks

Plain wooden blocks are available in a variety of shapes and sizes from many suppliers. For this project we used fifteen 5cm (2in) blocks but any shape or size will work – just adjust your templates accordingly.

YOU WILL NEED ✿ patterned scrapbook papers ✿ square wooden blocks ✿ ruler ✿ pencil ✿ scissors ✿ soft paintbrush ✿ découpage medium or PVA glue diluted with water to the consistency of thin cream ✿ greaseproof paper or baking parchment ✿ emery board or fine sandpaper ✿ water-based matt or gloss varnish

1 **Select a variety of scrapbook papers** to suit your colour scheme or theme. Measure the sides of the blocks.

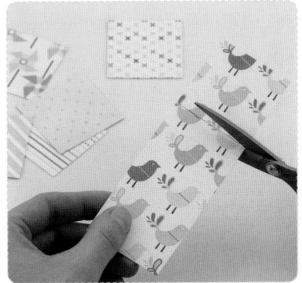

2 **Measure and mark** a piece of scrapbook paper to fit each side of the block. Cut the papers to size with scissors – you need six squares to cover one block.

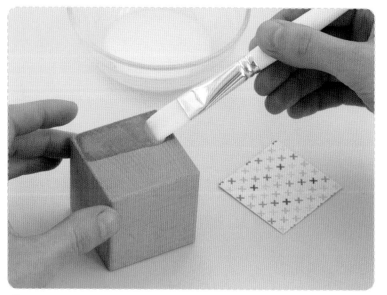

3 **Use a soft paintbrush** to apply découpage medium or diluted PVA glue to one side of the block and to the back of a paper square. Make sure both are thoroughly covered so there are no unglued areas.

4 **Position the glued paper** on the side of the block and smooth out the paper to remove any air bubbles.

5 **Coat the paper** with a layer of glue to seal it, then turn the block and repeat the process until you have covered all but one side.

6 **Leave the block to dry,** unpapered side down, on greaseproof paper or baking parchment.

7 **Once the block is dry,** glue paper to the last side and leave to dry again.

8 **Sand the edges** and corners of the blocks with an emery board or fine sandpaper. This bevels the edges, softens the corners, and creates a gently aged look.

emery board

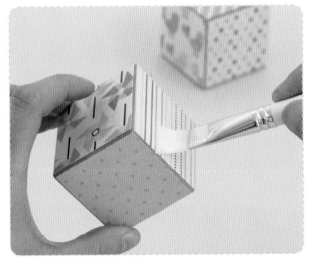

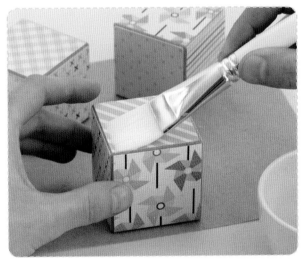

9 **Coat the block** with one or two more layers of glue to seal the paper. Pay special attention to the edges of the paper to make sure they don't lift from the block.

10 **To protect the paper** and create an attractive finish, apply a few coats of clear varnish – matt or gloss, depending on the effect you want. Allow each coat to dry before applying the next.

Sleepy puppy rattle

This rattle is easy for little hands to grip. You can embroider any facial expression on the rattle you wish or use the stitch guides provided on the template. Embroider a wide-awake puppy if you prefer.

YOU WILL NEED ✿ tracing paper ✿ pencil ✿ scissors ✿ small embroidery hoop ✿ 20 x 24cm (8 x 9½in) body fabric ✿ navy blue embroidery thread ✿ embroidery needle ✿ 12 x 28cm (4¾ x 11in) ear fabric ✿ pins ✿ sewing machine ✿ thread to match the fabric ✿ toy filling ✿ washable toy rattle less than 2.5cm (1in) in diameter ✿ needle ✿ iron

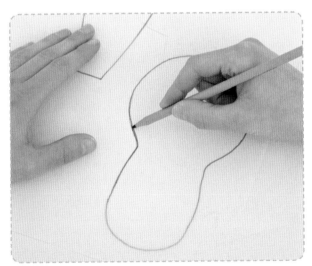

1 **Trace the templates** on page 236 onto tracing paper and cut them out to make the pattern pieces.

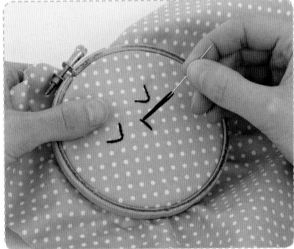

2 **Using an embroidery hoop,** needle, and thread, and following the stitching techniques on pages 224–225, embroider a face onto the body fabric. Make sure there is plenty of fabric around the embroidered face to position the pattern piece for the body.

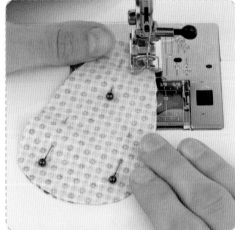

3 **Pin the pattern pieces to the fabrics** and cut them out. Cut four ears and two bodies, positioning the pattern piece for one of the bodies so it sits over the embroidered face, as shown. Make sure the face is centred within the head area before cutting.

4 **Pin two ears together,** right side to right side. Leaving the straight edge unstitched, sew around the curved edge, leaving a 5mm (¼in) seam allowance. Repeat to make the second ear.

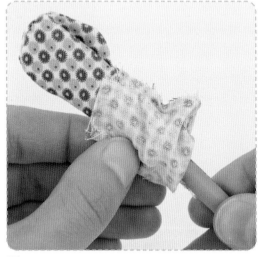

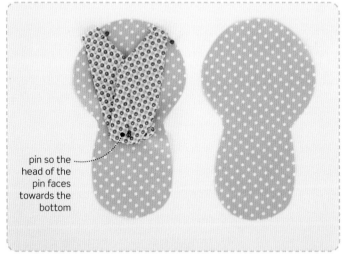

pin so the head of the pin faces towards the bottom

5 **Turn the ears to the right side** through the unstitched edge, using the blunt end of a pencil to push out the seams. Iron both ears.

6 **Pin the ears on top of one body,** right side up, as shown. Make sure they are exactly even along the curve of the head so that they will be level once sewn. Ensure that the edges of the ears align perfectly with the edge of the body.

7 **Pin the second body** right side down on top, aligning all the edges. Sew around the edges, leaving a 5mm (¼in) seam allowance and removing the pins holding the two bodies together as you sew. Leave a 2.5cm (1in) hole in one of the straight sides of the body. Clip into the seam allowances around all the curves.

8 **Carefully reach inside the body** to remove the pins holding the ears in place, then turn the body right side out through the hole. Stuff the rattle with toy filling and insert a rattle through the hole, pushing it up into the head.

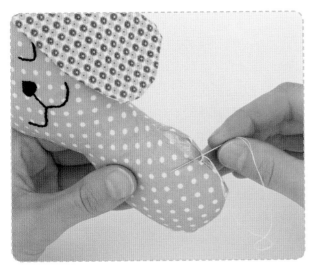

9 **Hand-stitch the hole closed** with a needle and matching thread, making small stitches that will be as invisible as possible.

Rolling woollies

These balls are made using a simple wet-felting technique. The finished balls are surprisingly light and tactile – perfect for little hands. Choose wool roving in the colour or colours of your choice. Many suppliers offer packs of wool roving in a variety of colours that work well together.

YOU WILL NEED ❂ merino wool roving, approximately 50g (1¾oz) per ball ❂ washing-up liquid ❂ medium to large bowl ❂ felting needle (optional) ❂ small amounts of wool roving in complementary colours (optional)

pull off small tufts of wool

roll the tuft into a small ball

1 **Fill a bowl with hot, soapy water** and set aside. The temperature should be as hot as your hands can comfortably bear. Find the end of the wool roving and pull off small tufts. The tufts will separate from the main piece of wool as you pull on them.

2 **Roll one tuft of wool** into a small ball, then roll a second tuft around it, alternating the direction of the fibres. Do this two to three times more, keeping the ball small and tidy. Set the extra tufts aside.

3 **Place a small drop** of washing-up liquid in your left hand. Using your right hand, dip the ball into the bowl of hot, soapy water. Soak the wool completely but do not let the tufts come apart.

4 **Roll the ball lightly** between your hands. Continue to roll in a circular motion for a few minutes until the ball is firm, indicating that the wool fibres of the tufts have bonded together.

5 **Wrap the ball** in another tuft and repeat steps 3 and 4. Continue to build up the layers, alternating the direction of the fibres as in step 2. Dip the ball in hot water and use more washing-up liquid, as necessary. The larger your ball gets, the longer the tufts of roving must be to wrap around.

felting needle

6 **Once your ball has reached** a suitable size, approximately 7–8cm (2¾–3in), rinse it under warm water to remove the washing-up liquid. Make sure the finished ball is large enough that it is not a choking hazard for baby. Leave the ball to dry on a surface you are not concerned about becoming stained, as some dye may leach out of the wool.

7 **Once the ball is dry,** you can add intricate designs using scraps of differently coloured wool roving. Lay the roving on the ball roughly in its final position, then work it into the ball by stabbing straight up and down with a felting needle. This bonds the fibres together. Add more wool as needed to achieve the precise design you want.

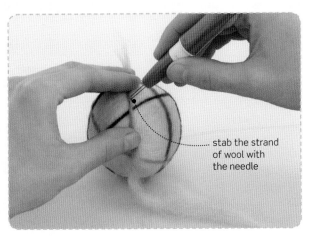

stab the strand
of wool with
the needle

To add a thin stripe to the ball, pull off a long, thin piece of wool roving in the colour of your choice. Twist the strands into a thin thread and place it on the ball. Work a small section into the ball with the felting needle. When that section is well-bonded, move on to the next. Make sure all the pieces of roving are firmly incorporated into the ball and cannot be pulled off by your baby.

TOP TIP *If the water cools, replace it with fresh hot, soapy water.*

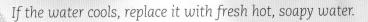

Nature-themed stacking rings

Stacking rings help to improve baby's coordination. These felt rings are playful depictions of objects from nature in colours that echo the colours of the rainbow. Use the embroidery stitches on pages 224–225 to embellish your rings.

YOU WILL NEED ❀ tracing paper ❀ marker pen ❀ scissors ❀ light blue, dark blue, yellow, red, black, orange, purple, dark green, and bright green felts ❀ pins ❀ embroidery needle ❀ embroidery threads in colours to match the felts ❀ toy filling ❀ pencil ❀ ruler

1 **Trace the templates** on page 244 onto the tracing paper and cut them out to make the pattern pieces.

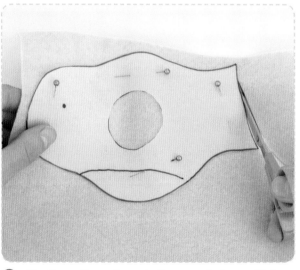

2 **Pin the pattern pieces** to the correct pieces of felt, as labelled on the templates, then cut the felt out.

3 **Use embroidery thread** to sew the details to the body pieces – the belly to one bluebird piece; the head, wing, and spots to one of the red ladybird pieces; the orange sun to one yellow disc; and the yellow ring to one purple flower.

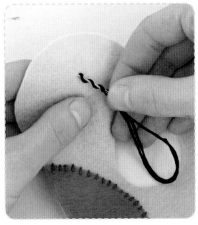

4 **Work the embroidered** details onto the body pieces, as indicated on the templates. Embroider the ladybird's eyes, the veins of the leaf, and the eye and tail details of the bluebird.

5 **With wrong side** to wrong side, match and pin together the two halves of each felt shape. Use blanket stitch (see p.224) and contrasting or coordinating thread to edge the hole in the centre of each stacking shape.

place the beak between the two halves and stitch in place ......

6 **With the felt halves still pinned together,** join the edges using blanket stitch, leaving a hole for stuffing. For the bluebird's beak and the stem of the leaf, sandwich the beak and stem in position between the two pieces of felt. Using a straight stitch, stitch the beak and stem in place, as shown.

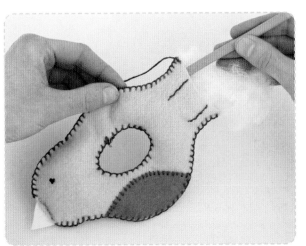

7 **Stuff the stacking shapes** with toy filling, using the blunt end of a pencil to work the filling around the central hole until the entire shape is stuffed with filling.

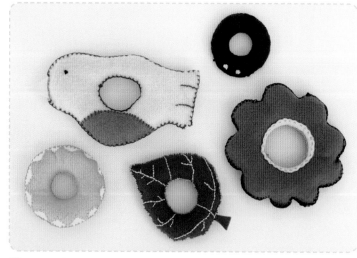

8 **Sew the hole for inserting** the stuffing closed using blanket stitch. The five stacking shapes should now be complete, as shown.

9 **Measure and mark** two 14 x 14cm (5½ x 5½in) squares and four 14 x 5cm (5½ x 2in) rectangles in bright green felt to make the base. Cut them out.

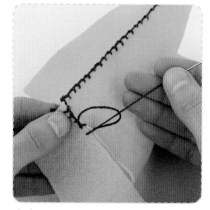

10 **Sew the sides** of the post together using blanket stitch, leaving the bottom open. Firmly stuff the post with toy filling. Centre the stuffed post on one of the 14 x 14cm (5½ x 5½in) green squares and sew it in place, tucking in the excess stuffing as you work so it does not stick out. This is now the top of the base.

11 **Sew one long edge** of each green rectangle to the top of the base using blanket stitch and contrasting thread. Sew three of the four pairs of short edges together, leaving one unsewn. Attach the remaining felt square – the bottom – to the free edges of the green rectangles using blanket stitch.

12 **Stuff the base** with toy filling through the open corner, then stitch the corner closed with blanket stitch.

Fabric animals picture book

A picture book made of fabric is ideal for young babies. It is soft, can be thrown in the wash, and will stand up to years of wear and tear. Make up your own stories to accompany the pictures or, as your baby grows, have them tell you stories about them.

YOU WILL NEED ✿ 69 x 46cm (27 x 18in) light-blue fabric for the pages ✿ ruler ✿ tailor's chalk ✿ scissors ✿ tracing paper ✿ marker pen ✿ pins ✿ scraps of fabric in an assortment of colours and prints for the motifs and binding ✿ sewing machine capable of zigzag stitch ✿ matching threads ✿ large-eyed needle ✿ black, pink, and blue embroidery threads ✿ iron

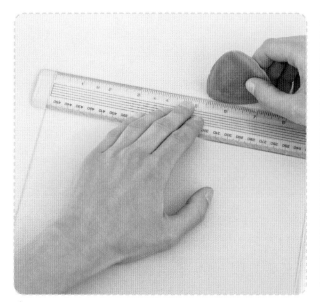

1 **Use a ruler, tailor's chalk, and scissors** to measure, mark, and cut out six 23 x 23cm (9 x 9in) squares of fabric, one for each page of the book.

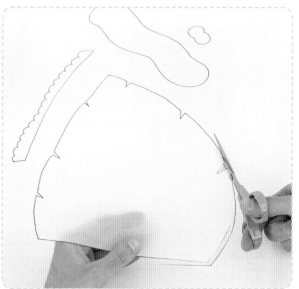

2 **Trace the templates** on page 248 onto the tracing paper and cut them out to make the pattern pieces.

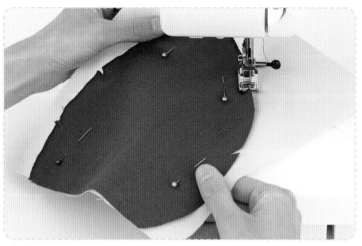

3 **Pin the pattern pieces** to the correct fabrics, as marked on the templates, and cut the fabric pieces out.

4 **Pin in place the first fabric piece** for each page, as numbered on the templates. Thread the sewing machine with matching thread and set it to a wide zigzag stitch with a short 0-1 stitch length, to create a neat satin stitch. Zigzag around the edges of the piece to attach it to the page.

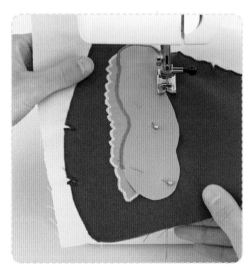

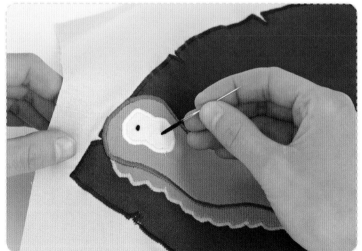

5 **Pin the second piece** in place and use matching thread to zigzag around its edge. Repeat for the remainder of the pieces, working in numerical order.

6 **Once all the pieces are attached** with satin stitch, use a large-eyed needle and embroidery thread to embroider the details, as marked on the template. Thread the machine with pink thread to sew the satin stitch inside the rabbit's ears and the frog's mouth.

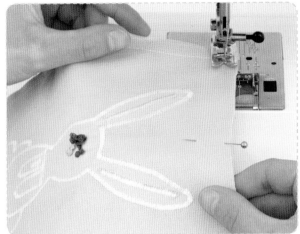

7 **With the pages now complete,** arrange them in the order you'd like them to appear in the book. Page one will be the front cover of the book; pages two and three will be facing each other; pages four and five will be facing each other; and page six will be the back cover. Iron all the pages.

8 **Trim each page** so that it is 21cm (8½in) square. Place pages one and two right side to right side with their motifs facing the correct way up. Leaving a 1cm (½in) seam allowance and with a straight stitch of normal length, sew around three sides, leaving the side that will be bound inside the spine unsewn. Repeat with the third and fourth pages, then with the fifth and sixth.

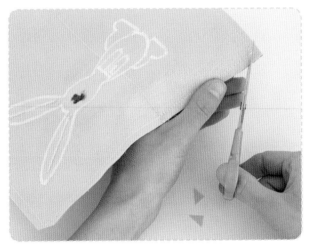

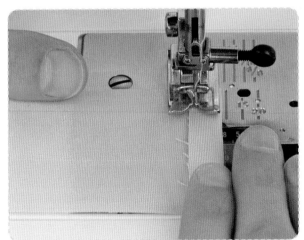

9 **Trim the two outer corners** of each pair of pages on the diagonal, being careful not to cut through the stitches. Turn each pair of pages to the right side through the unsewn side, then iron.

10 **Cut a piece of fabric** 21 x 8cm (8½ x 3in) for the binding. Fold the short, 8cm (3in), edges under by 1cm (½in), wrong side to wrong side. Use a straight stitch to sew them in place.

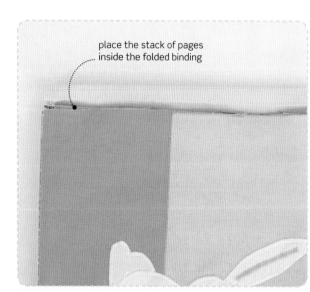

place the stack of pages inside the folded binding

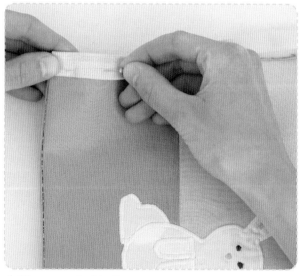

11 **Fold both long edges** under by 1cm (½in) and iron along the folds. Stack the book pages together, all the right way up and with their raw edges all facing the same direction. Place the raw edges inside the folded binding.

12 **Wrap the binding** around the raw edges of the pages and pin it in place. Make sure the edges of the pages and the top and bottom edges of the binding align with one another.

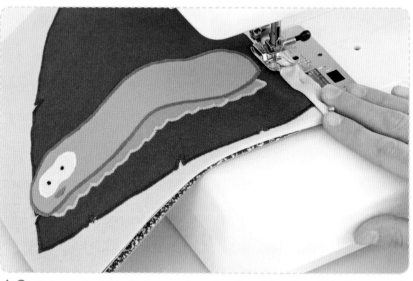

13 **Using a straight stitch,** sew along the edge of the pinned binding, through all the pages and through both sides of the binding, to hold the book together.

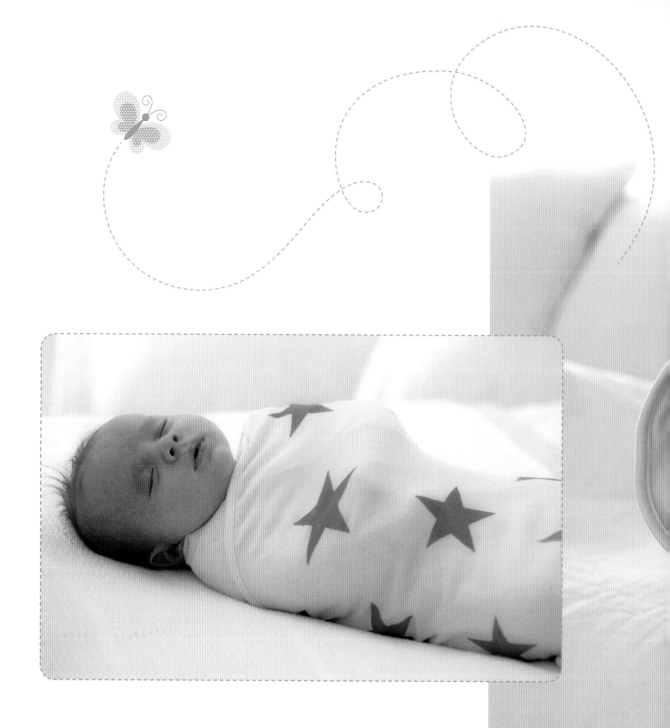

Starry night swaddle blanket

see pages 66-69

Squashy octopus

Let this lovable, cuddly octopus brighten up your nursery. His floppy tentacles and squishy body make him incredibly endearing. If you like, you could put a noise-making toy notion inside each tentacle.

YOU WILL NEED ❀ tracing paper ❀ marker pen ❀ scissors ❀ 30.5 x 40.5cm (12 x 16in) body fabric ❀ 16 scraps of different 8 x 18 (3 x 7in) fabrics for the tentacles ❀ 18 x 18cm (7 x 7in) bottom fabric ❀ fusible interfacing (optional) ❀ pins ❀ sewing machine ❀ matching thread ❀ needle ❀ toy filling ❀ large-eyed needle ❀ navy and white embroidery threads

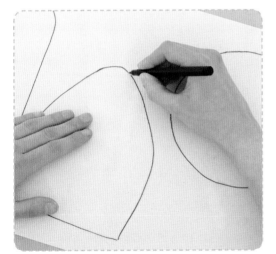

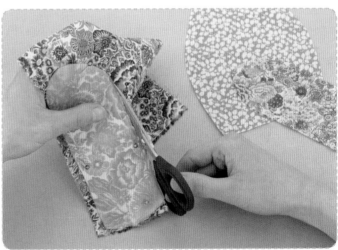

1 **Trace the templates** on page 237 onto the tracing paper and cut them out to make the pattern pieces.

2 **Pin the pattern pieces to the fabrics** and cut them out. If your fabric is lightweight, you may wish to reinforce it with fusible interfacing before cutting it out. Cut four body pieces from the same fabric; one bottom, circular piece in a contrasting fabric; and 16 tentacle pieces. Here we have cut eight pieces from different fabrics for the upperside of the tentacles and eight pieces from the same fabric for the underside of the tentacles.

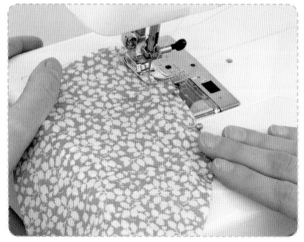

3 **Place two body pieces together,** right side to right side. Pin together down the right-hand edge. Leaving a 5mm (¼in) seam allowance, sew along the pinned edge from top to bottom, leaving the other edge and the bottom unsewn.

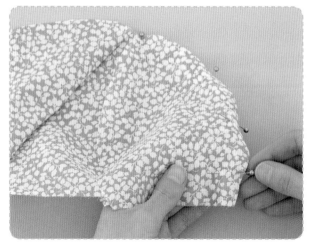

4 **Open up the two pieces** and, right side to right side, pin another body piece to the free right-hand edge. Sew along this pinned edge, making sure not to catch the other body piece in the stitching. Repeat to attach the fourth body piece.

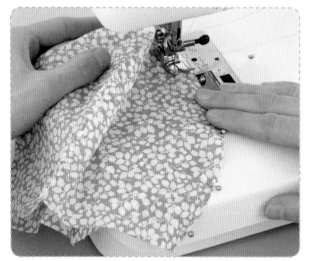

5 **Pin the two free edges together,** right side to right side. Sew along the pinned edge from top to bottom. You now have a complete cone shape, open at the bottom, for the octopus body.

6 **Using a needle and thread,** sew a few stitches through the top of the cone, where the four body pieces join. This will close any gap in the top and will ensure that the body pieces stay together. Set the body aside.

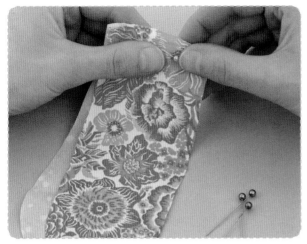

7 **Match an upperside** and an underside of a tentacle, right side to right side, to make a pair. Pin together.

8 **Leaving a 5mm (¼in) seam allowance,** sew around the outer edge of the tentacle, leaving the bottom, straight edge open. Clip into the seam allowance around the curved section of the tentacle.

9 **Turn the tentacle** right side out, iron, and lightly stuff with toy filling through the open bottom edge. For the time being, push the filling right to the bottom of the tentacle so it will be easier to sew on. Repeat steps 7–9 to make the remaining seven tentacles.

10 **Place the open edge** of a tentacle to the edge of the bottom circle and pin it in place, underside tentacle fabric to right side of circle fabric. Leaving a 1cm (½in) seam allowance, sew the tentacle to the circle. Repeat with the other tentacles, working in a clockwise direction around the circle and making sure that each tentacle sits right up against its adjacent tentacle. Repeat until all eight tentacles have been sewn onto the circle.

11 **When all the tentacles** have been sewn onto the circle, clip into the seam allowance all around the outer edge of the circle.

12 **With the conical body** still wrong side out, gather up all eight tentacles and insert them into the body. Ensure that the wrong side of the circle is facing outwards, towards the opening in the bottom of the body.

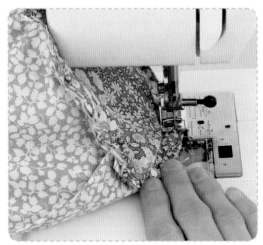

13 **Pin the bottom edge** of the body to the edge of the circle, right side to right side, spacing the pins quite close together. It is important to ensure that the circle fits evenly and flat against the edge of the body. Re-pin any areas where this is not the case. Having clipped the seam allowance in step 11, it should be easier to get the circle to lie flat.

14 **Leaving a 1cm (½in) seam allowance,** sew all the way around the pinned edges, leaving a hole about one and a half or two tentacles wide so that you can turn the octopus through and stuff it. Remove the pins as you work. Clip into the seam allowance all the way around.

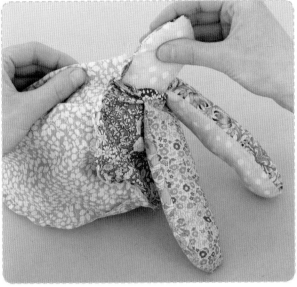

15 **Turn the octopus right side out,** pulling the tentacles through the hole first, then turning the body to the right side.

16 **Firmly stuff the octopus body** with toy filling and sew the hole closed.

17 **Thread a large-eyed needle** with embroidery thread and, using satin stitch and back stitch (see pp.224–245), embroider two eyes and a mouth on the octopus' body.

Flutterby pram toy

Hang this butterfly, with its crinkly wings, from your baby's pram or car seat. When choosing your fabrics, go for eye-catching colours and patterns.

YOU WILL NEED ❀ tracing paper ❀ pencil or marker pen ❀ scissors ❀ 14 x 18cm (5½ x 7in) body fabric ❀ 22 x 42cm (8½ x 16½in) wing fabric ❀ 56 x 22cm (22 x 8½in) fusible interfacing ❀ iron ❀ pins ❀ sewing machine ❀ matching thread ❀ 21 x 21cm (8¼ x 8¼in) cellophane ❀ black embroidery thread ❀ embroidery needle ❀ 30cm (12in) of 5mm (¼in) wide ribbon ❀ toy filling ❀ needle

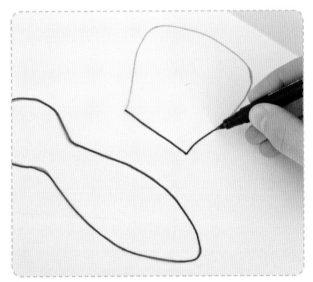

1 **Trace the templates** on page 236 onto the tracing paper and cut them out to make the pattern pieces.

2 **Lay the fusible interfacing** shiny side down on the wrong side of both the body and the wing fabrics. Iron with a cool iron to join the interfacing and fabric together.

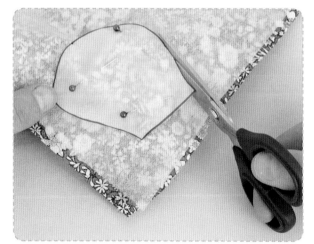

3 **Pin the pattern pieces** to the correct pieces of fabric and cut them out. Cut a total of eight wings and two bodies but reverse the pattern piece when cutting four of the wings, so you end up with four pairs.

4 **Pin two wings together,** right side to right side. Leaving the straight edge unstitched, sew around the curve, leaving a 5mm (¼in) seam allowance. Clip into the seam allowance around the curve. Turn the wing right side out through the unstitched edge and iron.

5 **Cut a piece of cellophane** to fit flat inside the wing and insert it through the unstitched edge. The cellophane will make the wing crinkly. Repeat steps 4 and 5 to make the three remaining wings.

6 **Using embroidery thread,** embroider two French knots (see p.224) at the head end of each of the bodies to make the butterfly's eyes. Use the main photograph as your guide.

7 **Fold the ribbon** in half and tie a secure knot in the end. For the antennae, cut two 13cm (5in) lengths of embroidery thread, fold in half and tie several knots at the end, one knot on top of the other, to make a large knot. Tie one knot in the other end of each thread.

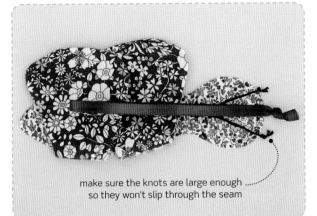

make sure the knots are large enough
so they won't slip through the seam

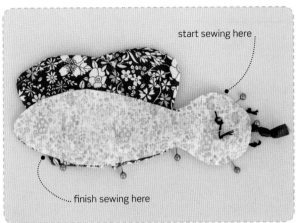

start sewing here

finish sewing here

8 **Lay one body right side up,** then place two wings
on top so their raw edges slightly overhang one side
of the body. Make sure the wings are the right way
up, as marked on the template. Place the ribbon in
the centre of the head with the knot overhanging.
Place the two antennae on either side of the ribbon
with their big knots also overhanging, as shown.

9 **Place the second body on top,** right side down,
and pin it in place along one side, as shown. Sew
around the pinned area only, leaving a 5mm (¼in)
seam allowance. Forward- and reverse-stitch over
the ribbon and antennae several times to secure
them in place. Remove the pins as you work.

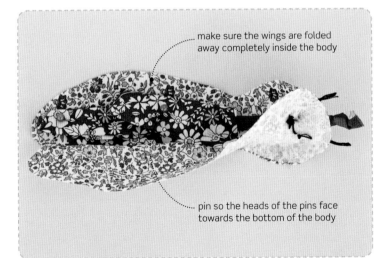

make sure the wings are folded
away completely inside the body

pin so the heads of the pins face
towards the bottom of the body

10 **Fold the wings twice** so they sit inside the body and pin
them in place. It is important that the heads of the pins all
face towards the bottom of the butterfly's body, so you can
remove them later.

11 **Fold the other two wings** twice and
pin to hold the folds in place.

12 **Place these two wings** on the opposite side of the body so their raw edges slightly overhang the other side of the body. Pin them in place, as shown. Make sure the wings are the right way up, as marked on the template, and that all your pin heads inside are facing towards the bottom of the butterfly's body.

13 **Fold the second body back,** aligning the edges of the two bodies all around. Pin in place. You may find it easier to align the edges if you bend the pins slightly.

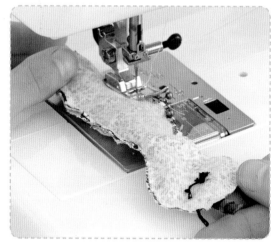

14 **Leaving the bottom** of the butterfly's body open, sew around the pinned edge to the start of the seam that was sewn in step 9. Leave a 5mm (¼in) seam allowance. Be sure not to catch the folded wings in your stitches.

15 **Use your finger to carefully remove** the pins from the wings inside the body, then turn right side out. Press with a cool iron so as not to melt the cellophane. Stuff the butterfly's body with toy filling, then hand-stitch the bottom closed. Make sure all pieces are firmly sewn on and the ribbon does not present any hazard.

Floppy mouse toy

No toddler could resist carrying around this cuddly mouse with his gangly arms and legs and his large, floppy ears. Choose hard-wearing fabrics such as heavy-weight cottons so your mouse will stand the test of time.

YOU WILL NEED ✿ tracing paper ✿ marker pen ✿ scissors ✿ pins ✿ 26.5 x 42cm (10½ x 16½in) fabric for body ✿ 61 x 42cm (24 x 16½in) fabric for head and extremities ✿ 28 x 20cm (11 x 8in) fabric for details ✿ pencil ✿ sewing machine ✿ matching thread ✿ toy filling ✿ thin paintbrush or chopstick ✿ needle ✿ large-eyed needle ✿ white and navy embroidery threads

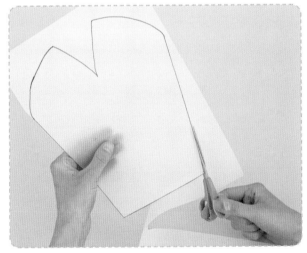

1 **Trace the templates** on page 245 onto the tracing paper and cut them out to make the pattern pieces.

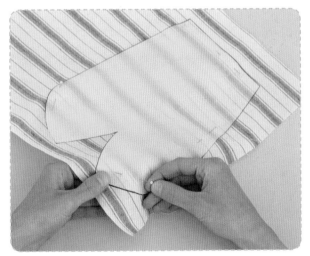

2 **Pin the pattern pieces** to the correct fabrics and cut them out following the instructions on the templates. In addition, draw and cut out two circles 5cm (2in) in diameter and a 4 x 21.5cm (1½ x 8½in) strip from the detail fabric for the tail. Finally, cut two 18 x 16.5cm (7 x 6½in) rectangles from the extremities fabric for the legs.

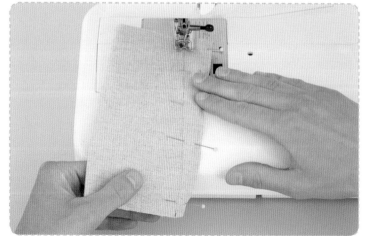

3 **Fold one of the** 18 x 16.5cm (7 x 6½in) leg rectangles in half lengthways, right side to right side. Align the edges and pin. Measure and mark 1cm (½in) from the aligned edges at one end of the rectangle and 5mm (¼in) at the other end. Lightly draw a line between the two marks, as shown. Sew along the line to make the leg seam, then trim the seam allowance to 5mm (¼in).

4 **Pin one of the 5cm (2in) circles** right side to right side inside the larger opening at one end of the leg.

5 **Leaving a 5mm (¼in) seam allowance,** sew around the edge, lifting the presser foot to rotate the fabric as necessary. Remove the pins as you work.

6 **Clip into the curved seam allowance,** turn the leg to the right side, iron, and stuff the leg lightly with toy filling. Pin and sew the top edge of the leg closed, leaving a 5mm (¼in) seam allowance and positioning the leg seam so that it sits at the back of the leg. Repeat steps 3–6 for the second leg.

7 **Fold the tail strip** in half lengthways and pin. Sew along one short end and along the long edge, leaving a 1cm (½in) seam allowance. Leave the other short end unsewn so that you can turn the tail right side out.

8 **Using a long, thin,** blunt tool, such as the handle of a thin paintbrush or a chopstick, turn the tail to the right side and iron.

9 **With one of the body pieces** right side up, position the tail inside the top of the dart. Fold the body piece over, right side to right side, sandwiching the tail in between. Pin along the dart, making sure the tail is caught in place between the edges of the dart.

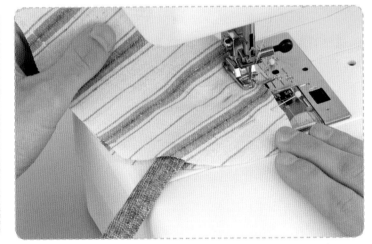

10 **Leaving a 5mm (¼in) seam allowance,** sew along the dart following the curve of the fabric. Forward- and reverse-stitch over the end of the tail a few times to make sure it is securely sewn in place and will not come out. This is the back of the mouse. Use the same method to sew up the dart on the other body piece to create the front of the mouse.

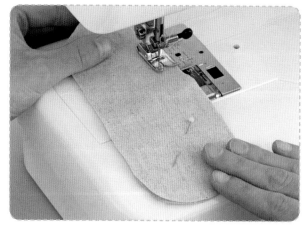

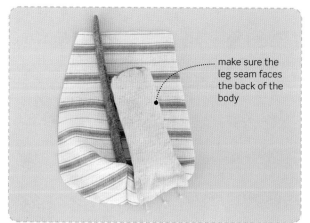

make sure the leg seam faces the back of the body

11 **Place two arm pieces** right side to right side and pin. Leaving the straight edge unsewn, sew around the edges with a 5mm (¼in) seam allowance. Clip into the seam allowance, turn to the right side, iron, and lightly stuff the arm with toy filling. Leaving a 5mm (¼in) seam allowance, pin and sew the open end closed. Repeat for the second arm.

12 **Lay the back of the mouse** right side up, with the tail tucked up towards the head. Pin one leg in place at the bottom of the back, as shown. Position the leg seam face down, so that when the leg is sewn in place, the seam will be at the back of the mouse. Leaving a 5mm (¼in) seam allowance, sew the edge of the leg to the body.

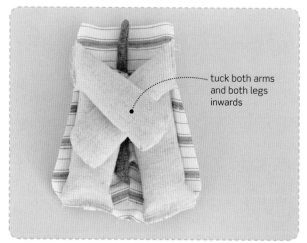

tuck both arms and both legs inwards

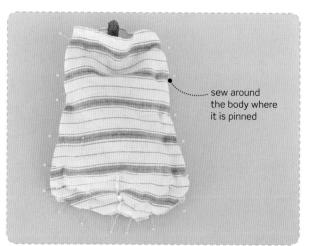

sew around the body where it is pinned

13 **Repeat for the second leg,** then add the two arms. Both arms and legs will now be sewn to the back of the mouse. Tuck the arms and legs inwards, as shown.

14 **Place the front of the mouse** right side down on top of the back of the mouse and the arms and legs. Align the edges and pin the front and back together, as shown. With a 1cm (½in) seam allowance, sew around the pinned edges, leaving the straight edge unsewn.

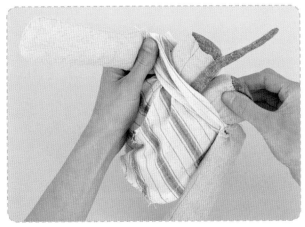

15 **Clip into the seam allowance** around the curves, then turn the body to the right side through the unsewn edge.

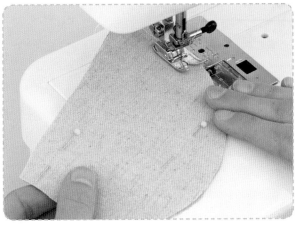

16 **Pin the two face pieces** right side to right side and sew around the curved edge only, leaving a 1cm (½in) seam allowance. Clip into the seam allowance around the curve, then turn the face to the right side.

17 **Pin two ear pieces together** right side to right side, one piece in the extremities fabric and one in the detail fabric. Leaving a 5mm (¼in) seam allowance, sew around the curved edge only. Clip into the seam allowance, turn the ear to the right side, and iron. Repeat for the second ear.

18 **Make a small fold of** approximately 5mm (¼in) in the bottom right-hand edge of what will be the left ear and another in the bottom left-hand edge of what will be the right ear, so that when the ears are in place, the folds are on the top of the mouse's head. Stitch the folds in place, then pin the ears on either side of the head. Stitch the ears to the head, leaving a 5mm (¼in) seam allowance.

19 **Turn the face wrong side out,** with the ears inside. Pin the back of the head to the face, right side to right side, along the curved edges. Sew along the curved edges leaving a 1cm (½in) seam allowance. Leave the bottom, straight edge open: this is the neck. Clip into the seam allowance around the curve, then turn the head to the right side.

20 **Pin the front edge of the neck** to the front of the body, right side to right side. Sew along the pinned edges, leaving a 1cm (½in) seam allowance.

21 **Stuff the mouse's body and head** with toy filling, then turn the raw edges at the back of the neck under by 1cm (½in). Using a needle and thread, sew the hole closed. Weave your needle back and forth to catch both edges of the fabric.

22 **Using a large-eyed needle** and navy and white embroidery threads, embroider a face on your mouse (see pp.224–225). Finish by tying a knot in the end of the mouse's tail.

Safari puppets

Take your baby on an African safari adventure as you tell him stories using these finger puppet characters. Or how about a pretend trip to the zoo? Use the head template to create your own characters to add to the menagerie.

YOU WILL NEED ❀ tracing paper ❀ marker pen ❀ scissors ❀ pins
❀ scraps of felt in light blue, pink, white, black, dark green, brown, and yellow
❀ needle ❀ matching threads

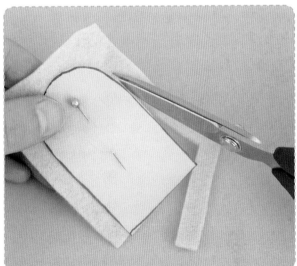

1 **Trace the templates** on page 243 onto the tracing paper and cut them out to make the pattern pieces.

2 **Pin the pattern pieces** to the correct pieces of felt, as indicated on the templates, and cut the felt out. Use the same head pattern piece for all four finger puppets, cutting two head pieces for each puppet.

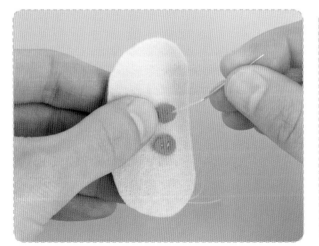

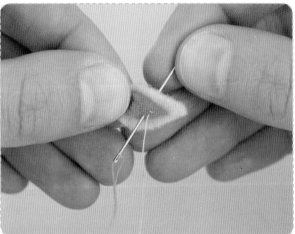

3 **Using a needle and matching thread,** start sewing the small face details in place on one head piece for each puppet. Sew the hippo's nostrils and teeth to his snout, sew the crocodile's teeth and eyes to his head, and sew the zebra's nose and stripes to his head.

4 **Continue to stitch** the small details in place using matching thread. Stitch the pink inner ear details to the ears for both the hippo and the zebra.

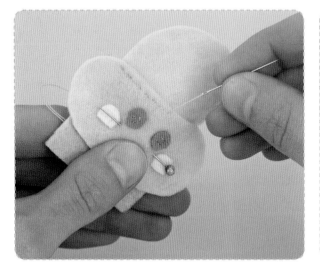

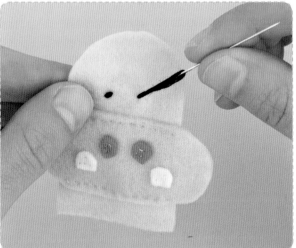

5 **Pin the large face details** to the heads and stitch them in place. Attach the hippo's snout, the lion's mane, and the zebra's ears. Only sew along the upper and lower edges of the hippo's snout and around the inner edge of the lion's mane.

6 **Using a needle and thread** and with the main photograph and templates as your guide, sew the facial features onto the animals. Give each animal a pair of eyes, sew small nostrils on the crocodile, and sew the face on the lion.

7 **Trim the thread tails** on the backs of all the pieces.

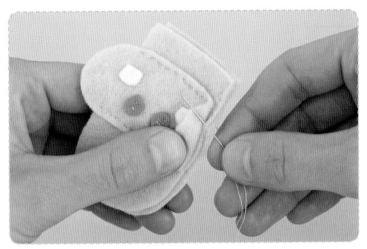

8 **Pair each finished animal's head** to a second head piece, matching the edges. Starting in one corner, use a needle and matching thread to sew the two head pieces together. As you go, lift up the edges of the hippo's snout and of the lion's mane so as not to catch them in the stitches.

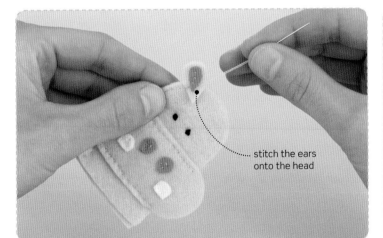

stitch the ears onto the head

9 **Continue to stitch** around the head pieces, sewing the hippo's ears in place as you stitch around the top of his head and sandwiching the zebra's mane between the two halves of his head. Continue until you have sewn all the way around to the other corner of each head, leaving the bottom edge open so that you can insert your finger.

10 **Your finger puppets** should now be complete. Due to their size, these finger puppets are intended for adult use only. Do not let babies or young children handle them as the small pieces can present a choking hazard.

Clothing

Set of baby bibs

You can never have enough baby bibs. This pattern is super-quick so it's easy to make several bibs. Use old or inexpensive towelling as the backing fabric. The pattern is designed for a six-month-old baby.

YOU WILL NEED ❀ tracing paper ❀ pencil ❀ scissors ❀ 28 x 21.5cm (11 x 8½in) cotton fabric per bib ❀ 28 x 21.5cm (11 x 8½in) towelling fabric per bib ❀ pins ❀ sewing machine ❀ matching thread ❀ iron ❀ needle ❀ approximately 8cm (3in) strip of Velcro®

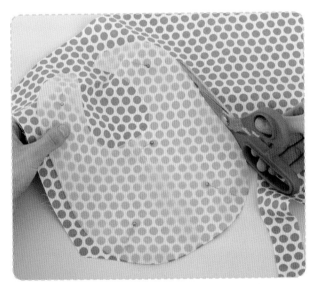

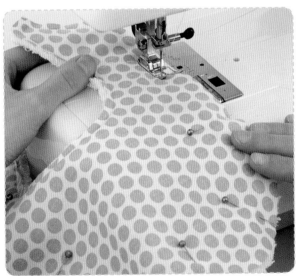

1 **Trace the template** on page 239 onto the tracing paper and cut it out to make the pattern piece. Pin the pattern piece to each fabric in turn and cut it out. For each bib, cut one in fabric and one in towelling.

2 **Place the fabric and towelling bib** right side to right side and pin them together. Leaving a 1cm (½in) seam allowance, stitch all around the edge apart from 7cm (2¾in) at the bottom edge for turning the bib through.

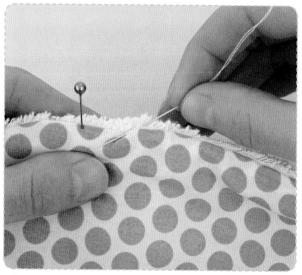

3 **Trim the seam allowance** along the curves to 5mm (¼in) and clip into it. Turn the bib right side out through the gap in the bottom edge.

4 **Iron the bib, then hand-stitch** the gap at the bottom closed, weaving your needle back and forth to catch the fabric on both sides.

5 **Cut a 2cm (¾in) strip of Velcro®.** Place one half of the Velcro® on the fabric side of the bib strap and stitch it in place. Place the other half of the Velcro® on the towel side of the opposite bib strap and sew it in place.

Enlarge the template if you'd like to make a bigger bib to fit an older child.

Summertime booties

These booties look fantastic with a little summer dress and are especially perfect for a special occasion. You can also make them for a boy: simply choose more masculine fabrics and ribbon.

YOU WILL NEED ✿ tracing paper ✿ pencil ✿ scissors ✿ pins ✿ 28 x 46cm (11 x 18in) main fabric ✿ 28 x 46cm (11 x 18in) lining fabric ✿ 13 x 15.5cm (5 x 6in) lightweight fusible interfacing ✿ iron ✿ sewing machine capable of zigzag stitch ✿ thread to match main fabric ✿ 80cm (32in) of 1cm (½in) coordinating ribbon ✿ thread to match your ribbon ✿ needle

1 **Trace the pattern templates** on page 235 onto tracing paper and cut them out to make the pattern pieces.

2 **Pin the pattern pieces** to the main and lining fabrics and to the interfacing. Cut out the number specified on the pattern templates. You can cut out the main and lining fabrics together to save time.

3 **Iron the sole interfacings** to the wrong side of the main fabric sole pieces, making sure they are centred.

4 **Place the main fabric and lining fabric fronts** right side to right side and pin them together. Stitch the top edge only, leaving a 5mm (¼in) seam allowance.

snip into the curves but do not cut through the stitches

5 **Trim the seam allowance** to 2.5mm (⅛in) and clip into the corners and curves. Turn the fronts right side out and iron.

6 **Place the main fabric and lining fabric backs** right side to right side and pin them together. Stitch around the top edges and sides leaving a 5mm (¼in) seam allowance. Trim the seam allowance to 2.5mm (⅛in) and clip the curves. Turn to the right side and iron.

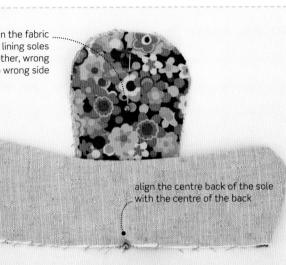

pin the fabric and lining soles together, wrong side to wrong side

align the centre back of the sole with the centre of the back

7 **Place the main fabric and lining fabric soles** wrong side to wrong side and pin. Pin the centre backs of the sole pieces to the centre of the backs, right side to right side, where indicated.

8 **Starting from the centre back,** continue pinning the backs to the soles, right side to right side.

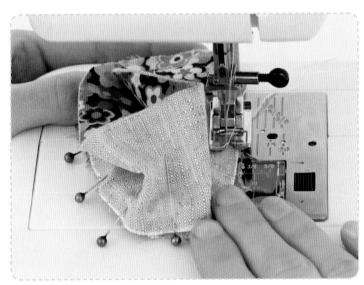

9 **Stitch the backs to the soles** leaving a 5mm (¼in) seam allowance and clipping carefully around the heel area as you sew, to make a smooth curve.

10 **Pin the front booties** to the soles right side to right side, matching the centre fronts of both pieces and overlapping the fronts on either side by 1cm (½in).

11 **Stitch the fronts in place,** then trim the seam allowances to 2.5mm (⅛in), clipping into the curves. Zigzag around the seams to neaten.

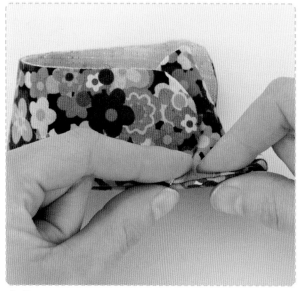

12 **Turn each bootie right side out** and, using your fingers, roll the seam to make the curve of the sole.

13 **Once finished,** cut the ribbon into four equal lengths and hand-stitch each length to the booties where indicated with an X on the pattern.

TOP TIP *Sewing small items can be tricky, so take your time as little mistakes will show.*

Rosette-embellished vests

Rosettes, or yo-yos as they're often called, are quick and simple to make and can be sewn to most things to add a cute touch. One of these vests can easily be made in less than an hour. Make sure the rosettes are securely attached so they won't come off in the wash or baby's hand.

YOU WILL NEED ✿ three vests or t-shirts in the size of your choice ✿ tracing paper ✿ pencil ✿ scissors ✿ pins ✿ scraps of lightweight fabric, at least 9 x 9cm (3½ x 3½in) each ✿ needle ✿ thread ✿ small embroidery hoop ✿ large-eyed embroidery needle ✿ green and charcoal embroidery threads ✿ five buttons

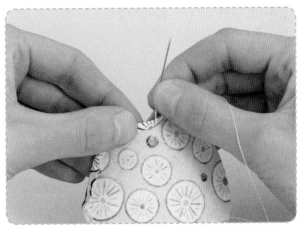

1 **Wash and pre-shrink** the vests or t-shirts. Trace the large, medium, and small rosette templates on page 233 onto the tracing paper and cut them out to make the pattern pieces. Pin the pattern pieces to the fabrics and cut out the rosettes you require for your project.

2 **To make a rosette,** thread your needle and securely knot the end of the thread. Working around the edge of a circle, fold approximately 3mm (⅛in) to the wrong side. Sew running stitches roughly 3mm (⅛in) in length along the folded edge, weaving your needle from front to back.

pull the thread to
gather the edges
of the circle

4 **When the rosette is evenly gathered,** take the
needle from the gathered side to the back and secure
with a knot. Ensure that the thread is tightly pulled
before making the knot so that the rosette remains
tightly and evenly gathered.

3 **Once you have sewn** all the way around the edge
of the circle, slowly pull on the thread to gather
the stitches and pull the circle into a rosette. Work
carefully so that the rosette gathers evenly and
the thread does not break.

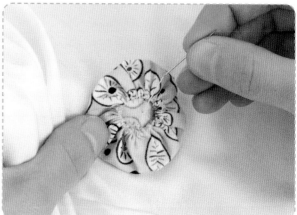

5 **Place the rosette** on the vest in the desired location,
using the main photographs as a guide. With your
needle and thread, securely sew the rosette to the
vest, working the stitches in the centre of the rosette.

Double rosette

1 **To make a double rosette,** follow steps 2–5 on pages 161–162 using a medium rosette. Stitch the rosette securely to the vest, taking care to catch only the back of the rosette to the vest without taking the stitches through to the front.

2 **Make a small rosette** and place this on top of the medium rosette. Stitch this securely in place as in step 5, opposite. Stitch the small rosette to the medium rosette, catching only the back of the small rosette.

3 **Position a button** in the centre of the small rosette. Use matching thread to attach the button securely, stitching through the centres of both rosettes and through the vest fabric.

Flower rosettes

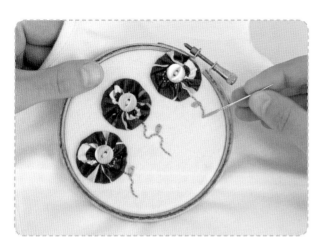

To make the flower rosettes, prepare three medium rosettes. Attach the rosettes and add the buttons to a vest using the techniques shown previously. Put the embroidery hoop over the area to be worked. Using the photograph and the embroidery stitch techniques on pages 224–225 as a guide, embroider the stems and leaves with green embroidery thread. Finally, remove the embroidery hoop and stitch down the edges of the rosettes.

Hot-air balloon

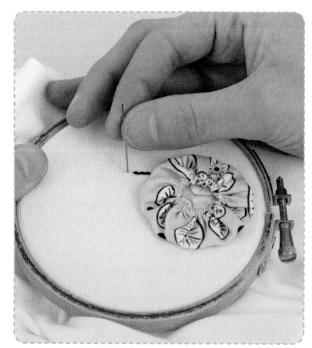

2 **Position the button** over the hole of the rosette. Using coordinating thread, stitch the button securely in place. Make sure it will not come off as it may present a choking hazard.

1 **For the hot-air balloon design,** make a rosette from a large circle. Position it correctly on the vest, then put the embroidery hoop over it on the area to be worked. Using the photographs and the embroidery stitch techniques on pages 224–225 as guides, embroider the hot-air balloon on the vest using a large-eyed needle and charcoal embroidery thread. Make sure the stitches for the cables sit just underneath the edge of the rosette. Once you have completed the design, secure the embroidery thread at the back.

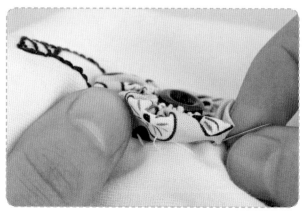

3 **Remove the embroidery hoop,** then stitch the rosette securely to the vest, taking care to catch only the back of the rosette to the vest without taking the stitches through to the front. Once you have stitched the rosette to the vest, secure the thread with a knot on the back of the rosette.

TOP TIP *Make sure the fabric is not pulled inside the hoop, or the stitches will be distorted.*

Sunny days bonnet

Perfect for sunny days in the garden or for a picnic, this cloth sun bonnet will fit a baby aged 9–12 months. Choose bright fabrics that complement one another for the main fabric and the lining.

YOU WILL NEED ❀ tracing or tissue paper ❀ pencil ❀ scissors ❀ pins
❀ 48.5 x 58.5cm (19 x 23in) cotton main fabric ❀ 48.5 x 51cm (19 x 20in) cotton lining fabric
❀ 18 x 35.5cm (7 x 14in) fusible interfacing ❀ iron ❀ sewing machine ❀ matching thread
❀ 25.5cm (10in) of 1cm (½in) elastic ❀ two safety pins

1 **Trace the pattern templates** on page 238 onto tracing or tissue paper and cut them out. Pin the pattern pieces to the fabrics and interfacing, as specified on the pattern. Cut them out.

2 **Iron interfacing** to the wrong side of the brim main fabric and to the brim lining fabric, making sure the interfacing is shiny side down. Follow the instructions that come with your interfacing when ironing it to the fabric.

3 **Fold and pin** the tie band pieces lengthways, right side to right side, as indicated on the pattern. Leaving a 1cm (½in) seam allowance, sew along the angled ends and long sides. Turn to the right side, then iron.

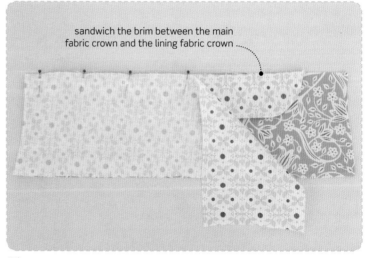

sandwich the brim between the main
fabric crown and the lining fabric crown ....

4 **Place the interfaced** brim pieces right
side to right side and stitch around
the edge, leaving a 1cm (½in) seam
allowance. Trim and clip the curves,
then turn to the right side and iron.

5 **Place the brim on the edge** of the main fabric crown, right side
to right side and matching the centres. Put the lining fabric crown
on top, matching the front edges and sandwiching the brim in
between. Stitch along the edge, through all the layers, then turn
through to the right side and iron.

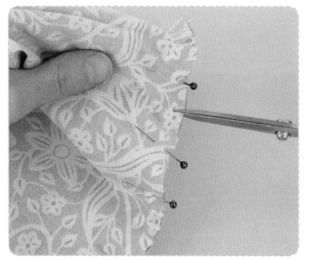

6 **Matching the markings** on the pattern, pin the main
fabric back to the free edge of the main fabric crown,
right side to right side. Make 5mm (¼in) snips along
the curved edge.

7 **Sew along the pinned curved edge** leaving a 1cm
(½in) seam allowance. Iron the seam towards the
centre of the bonnet. Repeat steps 6 and 7 to join
the lining back to the lining crown. Turn the bonnet
right side out.

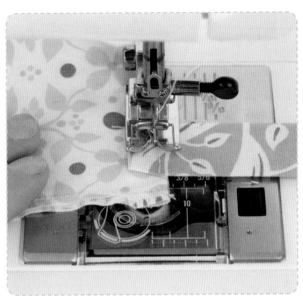

8 **Join the bottom edge** of the back by pinning the free edges of the main and lining backs together, matching the seams. Stitch along the entire length.

9 **Pin the tie bands** to the two front corners below the brim, 5mm (¼in) from the bottom edge. Position them so they stick outwards, as shown. Stitch them in place.

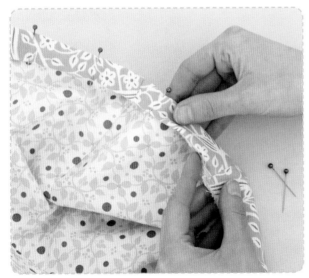

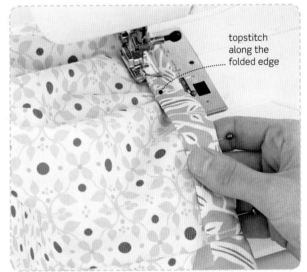

topstitch along the folded edge

10 **Fold up the bottom edge** 2cm (¾in) towards the lining of the bonnet, then fold it up again by the same amount. Pin in place.

11 **To form the casing for the elastic,** topstitch close to the edge of the first fold you made, removing the pins as you work.

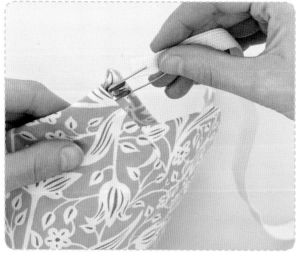

12 **With a safety pin on each end** of the elastic, thread it through the casing, so that the ends with their safety pins are just out of sight inside the casing.

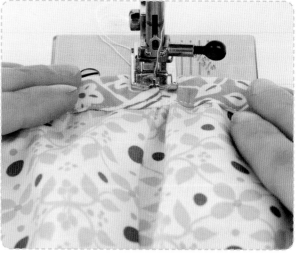

13 **Topstitch across the casing** over the seam where the back joins the crown on one side only: this will secure the elastic in place on that side of the bonnet.

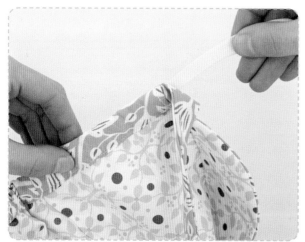

14 **Pull the other end of the elastic** to gather the fabric at the back of the bonnet. Sew across the casing over the other seam where the back joins the crown to secure the elastic in place on this side of the bonnet, as in step 13. Each end of the elastic will still have a safety pin attached to it.

15 **Pull on one of the safety pins** to pull the end of the elastic out of the casing. Cut the elastic as short as you can. The remaining elastic will spring back into the casing and no longer be visible. Repeat on the other side of the bonnet.

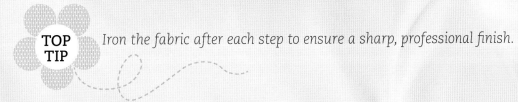

TOP TIP *Iron the fabric after each step to ensure a sharp, professional finish.*

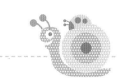

Selection of toys

see pages 96–99, 104–107, and 124–129

Sea-side stencilled vests

Using stencils made from freezer paper combined with fabric paints is a quick and easy way to dress up baby vests, t-shirts, or any other cloth items – the possibilities are endless. Use the stencil templates we've provided or design your own.

YOU WILL NEED ✿ freezer paper ✿ marker pen ✿ scissors ✿ craft knife ✿ cutting mat ✿ 1 baby vest per stencil ✿ iron ✿ cardboard ✿ fabric paints in bark blue, green, orange, red, purple, and white, or in the colours of your choice ✿ 1 paintbrush per colour, or wash your brush well between changes of colour

1 **Wash and pre-shrink** the items of clothing you plan to stencil. Trace the templates on page 241 onto the dull side of the freezer paper, leaving plenty of space around each design. Use scissors to cut out each design so it is centred on a rectangle of paper.

2 **Using the craft knife** and a cutting mat, cut away the freezer paper within the outlines to create each stencil.

iron on the dull side of the paper or it will melt and stick to your iron .....

3 **Centre the stencil,** shiny side down, on the front of the baby vest. Iron the stencil into position, making sure the fabric lies flat underneath. The stencil must be securely attached, especially around the cut edges of the design.

... avoid paint seeping through by placing cardboard behind the fabric

4 **Place a piece of cardboard** inside the vest, behind the stencil. This ensures that the paint will not bleed through. Use the white paint to mix lighter versions of the blue and purple paints, for the two-tone designs. Use the paintbrush to dab paint carefully and evenly over the stencil.

5 **Allow the paint to dry,** then apply a second coat. Leave to dry completely. If necessary, wash your paintbrush, then move on to the next stencil design.

6 **When the second coat is dry,** peel off the stencil. Finish as recommended by the paint manufacturer, usually by ironing. Wash and dry the stencilled fabric, following the manufacturer's instructions.

Rosette headband

A headband is a simple and pretty way to dress up a little girl. This headband is created using soft jersey fabric, so it is comfortable to wear. Choose a bright fabric and button to make your rosette so that it will really stand out.

YOU WILL NEED ❀ 7.5 x 58.5cm (3 x 23in) soft, cotton jersey fabric ❀ tape measure
❀ scissors ❀ pins ❀ sewing machine capable of zigzag stitch ❀ thread to match the fabric
❀ safety pin ❀ at least 38cm (15in) of 1cm (½in) wide elastic ❀ needle ❀ tracing paper
❀ pencil ❀ scrap of lightweight patterned fabric, at least 9 x 9cm (3½ x 3½in)
❀ 1 button, 2cm (¾in) in diameter ❀ thread to match the button

the fabric should stretch lengthways

1 **Ensure the jersey fabric** stretches lengthways, so that it will stretch around the child's head once it has the elastic threaded through.

2 **Fold and pin the fabric** in half, right side to right side, aligning the edges evenly. You should now have a strip 58.5cm (23in) long by 3.75cm (1½in) wide.

3 **Set your machine** to a wide zigzag stitch with a normal stitch length and sew along the fabric strip, 2cm (¾in) from the fold. The zigzag stitch will allow the fabric to stretch without the stitches breaking.

pull the tube
through to the
right side with
a safety pin

4 **Trim the seam allowance** to 5mm (¼in). Attach a safety pin to one end of the fabric tube and use this to turn the tube through, so that it is right side out (see p.226).

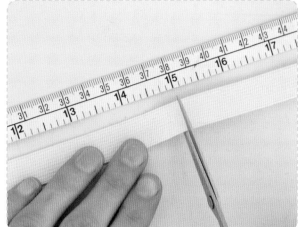

5 **Cut a length of elastic,** approximately 38cm (15in) long. You may want to make the elastic shorter or longer, depending on the circumference of the child's head as well as on how stretchy the elastic is. The elastic must stretch a little to go around the child's head but must not be too tight a fit.

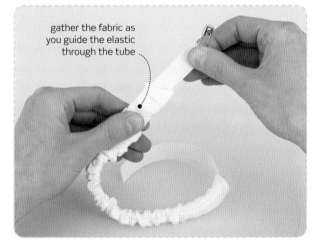

gather the fabric as
you guide the elastic
through the tube

6 **Attach a safety pin** to one end of the elastic and use the pin to thread the elastic through the fabric tube. You should finish with the ends of the elastic poking out from either end of the fabric tube and with the tube evenly gathered between.

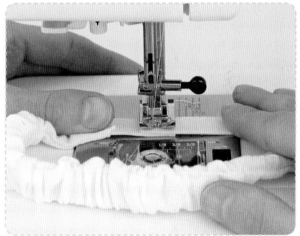

7 **Slightly overlap the two ends** of the elastic and stitch them together securely. To do this, work forward and reverse stitches over one another several times. After stitching the ends of the elastic, ease the fabric tube over the joined ends.

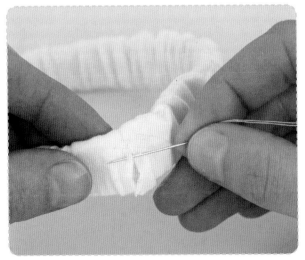

8 **Turn the ends of the fabric tube** to the inside. Line the ends up so they are not twisted, then hand-stitch together to close up the headband. Keep the seam flat to ensure it does not irritate the child's head.

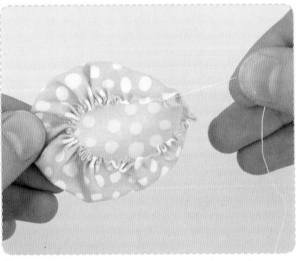

9 **Make a rosette** using the largest circle template on page 233 and following steps 1–4 on pages 161–162.

10 **Stitch the completed rosette** securely to the headband. If the headband seam is not completely flat, have it at the back of the child's head where it will irritate less. Otherwise position the seam more prominently and hide it with the rosette.

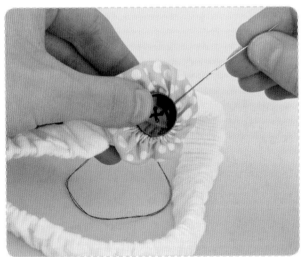

11 **Once the rosette is in place,** use matching thread to sew the button to the front of the rosette. Make sure the button is securely attached and will not come off as it may present a choking hazard.

Newborn cap

This soft, stretchy cap is designed to fit a newborn baby and matches the newborn mitts on pages 186–189. The two together would make a lovely gift set for any new baby. Choose appropriate fabrics depending on whether the baby is a girl or a boy.

YOU WILL NEED ✿ tracing paper ✿ pencil ✿ scissors ✿ 28 x 41cm (11 x 16in) soft, plain jersey fabric ✿ 25.5 x 41cm (10 x 16in) soft, patterned jersey fabric ✿ sewing machine capable of zigzag stitch ✿ ballpoint needle for the sewing machine (recommended) ✿ thread to match the fabrics ✿ pinking shears (optional) ✿ needle

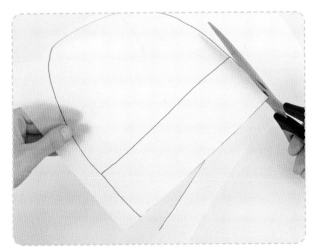

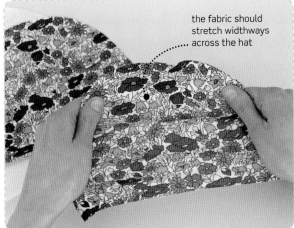

the fabric should stretch widthways across the hat

1 **Trace the template** on page 241 onto the tracing paper and use it to cut out one short pattern piece and one long pattern piece.

2 **Using the long pattern piece,** cut two pieces from the plain fabric. Using the short pattern piece, cut two pieces from the patterned fabric. Make sure you cut the fabric so that it stretches widthways across the hat, not lengthways.

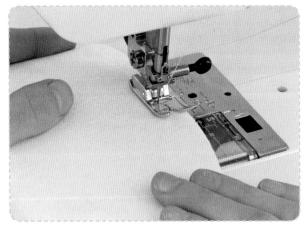

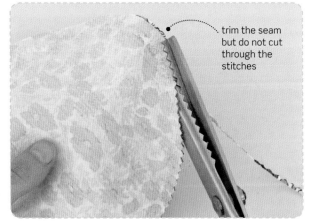

trim the seam but do not cut through the stitches

3 **Set the sewing machine** to a wide zigzag stitch with a normal stitch length. Place the plain fabric pieces right side to right side and, using a ballpoint needle, sew around the curve, 1cm (½in) from the edge. Trim the seam allowance to 5mm (¼in) and snip into the curve without cutting through the stitches. Or, use pinking shears to trim the seam allowance.

4 **Place the patterned fabric pieces** right side to right side and zigzag stitch around the curve, leaving a 1cm (½in) seam allowance. Trim and clip into the seam allowance as in step 3. Turn to the right side.

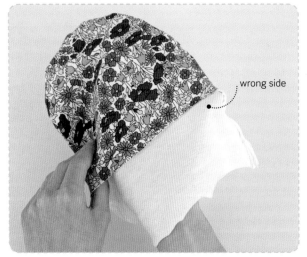

wrong side

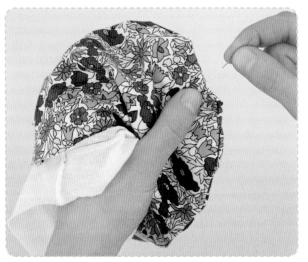

5 **Insert the plain fabric cap** into the patterned fabric cap, wrong side to wrong side. Align the seams and make sure the plain fabric cap sits smoothly and evenly inside the patterned fabric cap.

6 **Using a needle and thread,** sew a few stitches through the curved seams at the top of the cap to join the inner and outer caps together.

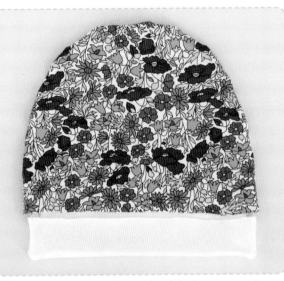

7 **Fold up the raw edge** of the plain inner cap twice, so that the first fold you made sits against the bottom edge of the outer patterned cap. Make sure the fold is even all around.

8 **Using a needle and thread,** securely stitch the folded edge of the inner cap to the outer cap, covering the raw edge of the outer cap.

Use soft fabrics that will sit comfortably against baby's sensitive skin. Organic bamboo jersey is a good choice for the inner cap.

Newborn mitts

Designed to match the newborn cap, these little mitts will stop your baby from accidentally scratching herself. Choose a soft, stretchy fabric so that they are comfortable against baby's delicate skin.

YOU WILL NEED ✿ tracing paper ✿ pencil ✿ pins ✿ scissors ✿ 23 x 25.5cm (9 x 10in) soft, jersey fabric ✿ sewing machine capable of zigzag stitch ✿ ballpoint needle for the sewing machine (recommended) ✿ matching thread ✿ 23cm (9in) of 5mm (¼in) wide elastic ✿ four small safety pins ✿ pinking shears (optional)

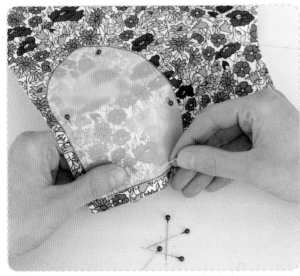

1 **Trace the template** on page 233 onto the tracing paper and cut it out. Pin this pattern piece to the fabric and cut around it. Repeat to make four identical mitt halves.

2 **Fold the straight edge** of one mitt half over by 3cm (1¼in) to the wrong side. Machine-stitch a straight line 5mm (¼in) from the edge, then another line, parallel to the first and 1.5cm (⅝in) from the edge, to form a casing. Repeat for the other three mitt halves.

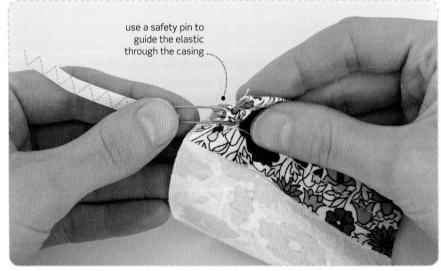

use a safety pin to
guide the elastic
through the casing

SIZE
To fit a
baby aged 0–3
months

3 **Cut four pieces of elastic,** each 5.5cm (2¼in) long. Attach a safety pin to
one end of each piece of elastic and use the pin to work the elastic part-way
through the casing.

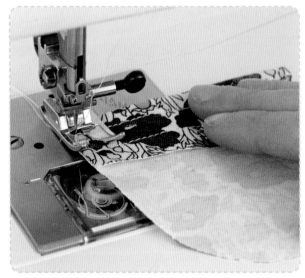

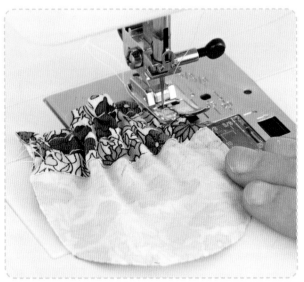

4 **Align the end of the elastic** without the safety pin
with the edge of the mitt. The remaining elastic will
be inside the casing. Sew the end of the elastic in
place with a few short machine stitches, first going
forwards then backwards.

5 **Continue working the remaining** elastic through
the casing, using the safety pin, so that the other end
of the elastic aligns with the other edge of the mitt
and the casing ruches. Remove the pin and, holding
the elastic, sew it in place, as in step 4. Repeat steps
4 and 5 for the remaining three mitt halves.

6 **Pin two mitt halves together** right side to right side, aligning the edges. Set the machine to a wide zigzag with a normal stitch length and sew around the curved sides of the mitt, close to the edge. Leave the elasticated edge open. Repeat for the second mitt.

7 **Trim the seam allowance** to 5mm (¼in) and snip into the curve without cutting through the stitches, or use pinking shears to trim the seam allowance. Finally, turn the mitt right side out. Repeat steps 6 and 7 for the second mitt.

When working with a stretch fabric, it is important to make sure you do not pull on the fabric when either cutting or sewing it, as it will distort the shape.

TOP TIP *A ballpoint needle prevents jersey fabric from tearing when you machine-sew it.*

Simple summer dress

This little dress is the simplest of shapes and is absolutely adorable.
The pattern is sized to fit a baby girl aged about one year.
Choose a bold and playfully patterned cotton fabric.

YOU WILL NEED ✿ tracing paper or dressmaking pattern paper ✿ pencil or marker pen
✿ scissors ✿ 1m (39½in) patterned cotton fabric ✿ pins ✿ 50 x 40cm (20 x 16in) fusible
interfacing ✿ iron ✿ sewing machine capable of zigzag stitch ✿ thread to match the fabric
✿ 2 press studs ✿ needle

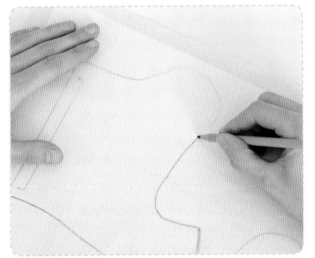

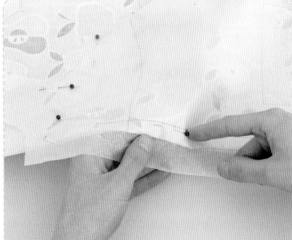

1 **Enlarge the templates** from page 240 as instructed, then trace them onto the tracing paper or dressmaking pattern paper. Cut them out.

2 **Pin the pattern pieces** to the fabric, as instructed on the templates. Make sure the pattern pieces are placed on the fold of the fabric where marked and that the pattern is the same way up on both main pieces of fabric. Cut out the fabric.

3 **Pin the front and back** facing templates to the interfacing and cut them out. Iron the interfacing to its corresponding fabric facing. Make sure the shiny side of the interfacing is against the wrong side of the fabric.

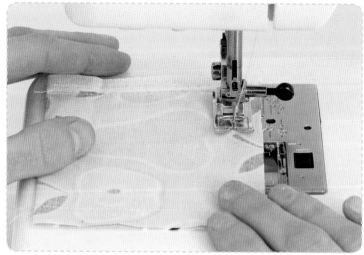

4 **Make the pocket** by folding the fabric right side to right side along the line indicated on the template. Leaving a 1cm (½in) seam allowance, stitch along all sides except the folded side. Leave a 2.5cm (1in) opening at the bottom of the pocket.

tease out the corners with a pin

5 **Turn the pocket** right side out through the opening. Carefully tease out the corners with a pin, then iron flat.

6 **Pin the pocket in place** on the front of the dress as indicated on the template, with the folded edge of the pocket at the top. Using the sewing machine, topstitch the pocket in place along its sides and along the bottom edge. Leave the top of the pocket open.

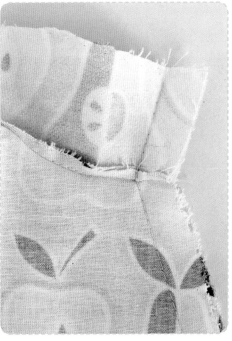

clip into the curve but
do not cut through
the stitches

7 **Lay the front facing** and the front dress together, right side to right side. Pin them together. Machine-stitch around the armholes and neck edges, leaving a 1cm (½in) seam allowance. Trim the seam allowance to 3mm (⅛in), then clip into the seam allowance with scissors to ease the curve, but do not cut through the stitches. Repeat for the back facing and the back dress.

8 **Turn the front and back** right side out and iron around the armholes and neck.

9 **Place the front and back** right side to right side and pin them together, opening up the interfaced facings. Mark the point where the facings open up with a pin. Stitch down the right side of the dress, pivoting slightly when you reach the pin, as shown above. Repeat on the left side of the dress.

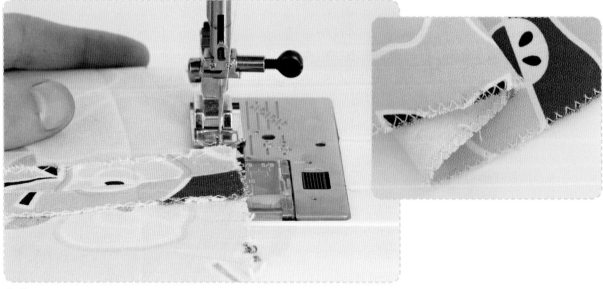

10 **Remove the pins** and set the machine to a wide zigzag with a
normal stitch length. Zigzag all the raw edges of the fabric and
the hem (see inset photo, above right).

11 **Fold up, pin, and iron** a 4cm (1½in) hem on the
bottom of the dress. The hem can be narrower or
wider, depending on the length you'd like the dress
to be. Machine-sew with a straight stitch 2.5cm (1in)
from the folded edge to secure the hem in place.

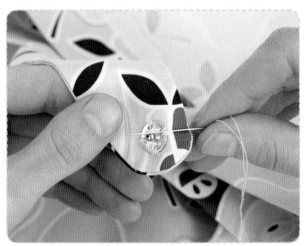

12 **Hand-stitch press studs** to the shoulder tabs,
so that the front tab overlaps the back tab.

For mum

Fingerprint pendant

Capture your baby's tiny fingerprint in a silver charm forever.
Baby's finger won't leave a clear print until he is at least six months
old, so this pendant is best made as a first birthday keepsake.

YOU WILL NEED ❀ oil (cooking spray is ideal) ❀ Teflon® sheet or greaseproof paper ❀ small rolling pin
❀ 10g (¼oz) silver clay ❀ playing cards ❀ small heart cutter (or template and craft knife)
❀ small drinking straw ❀ small star stamp ❀ cling film ❀ airtight container ❀ mirror
❀ sanding pads (180, 220, and 280 grit) ❀ ceramic tile or firing brick ❀ kitchen blowtorch ❀ timer
❀ tweezers ❀ small dishes ❀ liver of sulphur ❀ 2 pairs of pliers ❀ silver jump ring ❀ silver chain

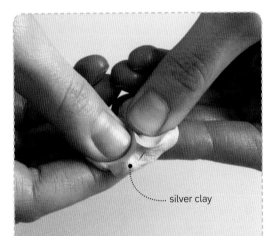

...... silver clay

...... Teflon® sheet or
greaseproof paper

1 **Prepare a non-stick work surface** by rubbing
a small amount of oil over the Teflon® sheet or
greaseproof paper. Lightly oil the rolling pin and
your hands, too. Gently knead the silver clay
between your fingers. It will be sticky at first
but can dry out quickly, so don't overwork it.

2 **Place two stacks of playing cards** (six cards in each stack)
about 5cm (2in) apart on the non-stick surface. These will
act as rolling guides to ensure that you roll your clay out to
a uniform thickness. Place the clay between the stacks of
cards and roll it out; it should have a clean, smooth finish.

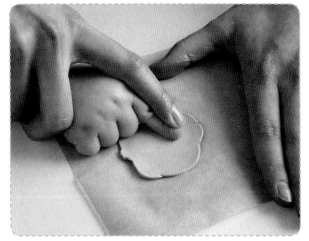

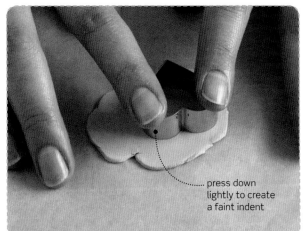

... press down
lightly to create
a faint indent

3 **Gently but firmly press** baby's finger into the clay so that it leaves a clear imprint. To get a clearly defined fingerprint, the baby will need to be at least six months old. If you do not get a good imprint, re-roll the clay and try again, but take care that the clay does not begin to dry out.

4 **Use the heart cutter** to lightly mark where you are going to cut the clay. Position it so the fingerprint is where you want it to appear on the charm. The indent from the cutter will help you to place your star motifs correctly. If you try and stamp the clay with stars after cutting, it will distort the shape of the charm.

5 **Using the drinking straw,** make a hole in the heart about 3mm (⅛in) from the edge. This hole must be big enough for your jump ring to move freely in it. Bear in mind that the clay will shrink by approximately 10 per cent during the firing process.

6 **Press the star stamp** firmly into the clay in the arrangement that you want. Try to press the stamp into the clay to the same depth each time so that all the star imprints will have the same clearly defined, even appearance.

TOP TIP

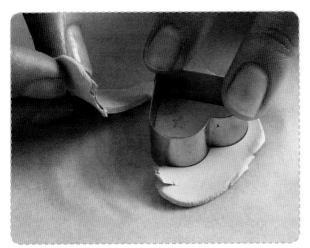

make sure no condensation
marks appear on the mirror

7 **Cut the heart out** by positioning the cutter over the indent made in step 4. Remove the excess clay from around the cutter. Roll up any scraps of clay and store them in clingfilm in an airtight container for future use. If the clay is starting to dry out, brush it lightly with water before storing.

8 **Leave the clay to dry overnight** or, to speed up the process, you can use a hair dryer or put the clay in an oven at 150°C (300°F/Gas 2) for 10 minutes. The clay must be completely dry before firing. Make sure it is dry by putting it on a mirror: if any condensation appears, it means there is still moisture in the clay.

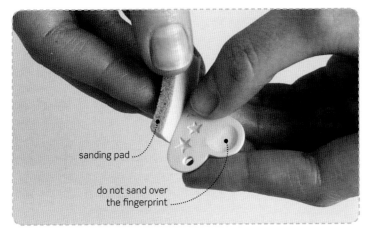

sanding pad

do not sand over
the fingerprint

9 **Once the clay is dry** it is extremely fragile, so be gentle. Sand the charm, starting with the 180 grit sanding pad. Next use the 220 grit sanding pad followed by the 280 grit one to achieve a smooth finish. Do not sand over the fingerprint. When you have finished, there should be no marks other than the fingerprint and the stars.

The more you work metal clay, the drier it becomes, so moisten it if any cracks appear.

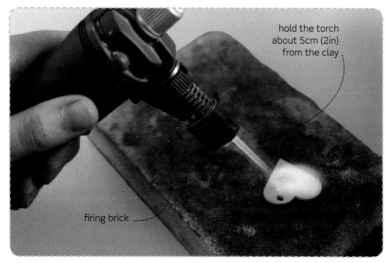

hold the torch
about 5cm (2in)
from the clay

firing brick

HOW TO FIRE THE CLAY

✿ To fire your metal clay you will
need to be in a well-ventilated,
dimly lit room.

✿ Have a dish of water, metal
tweezers, and a timer at hand.

✿ You will see a small flame and
smoke as the organic binder
burns away; this will only last
a few seconds.

✿ The clay will start to glow a
peachy-orange colour; you
need to maintain this colour
for two minutes.

✿ If it starts to glow bright red or
shiny silver, it is too hot, so
move the flame away slightly.

10 **Place the heart charm** on a ceramic tile or firing brick, on a heatproof
surface. Set the timer for two minutes. Hold the blowtorch about 5cm
(2in) from the clay and move the flame evenly over the charm. You will
see a small flame and smoke, then the clay will start to glow a peach
colour. Once it starts to glow, start the timer and continue firing.

liver of sulphur

11 **When the two minutes are up,** either leave
the charm to cool on the tile or carefully lift
it with the tweezers and place it in a dish of
cold water. The heart will now be a matt-white
colour, even though it is made of pure silver.

12 **Before polishing the charm,** you must patinate it to
highlight the fingerprint and the stars. Put a couple of
drops of the liver of sulphur in hot, but not boiling, water.
Then, using tweezers, place the charm in the solution.
The silver will quickly turn black. Once it is completely
black, use the tweezers to remove it, then wash it in
clean water and dry it.

do not sand the black finish off the fingerprint and stars

13 **To remove the black finish,** sand the charm again, once more working through the sanding pads from the 180 grit to the finest, the 280 grit. The longer you spend carefully sanding, the better the results will be. The black finish should remain in the details.

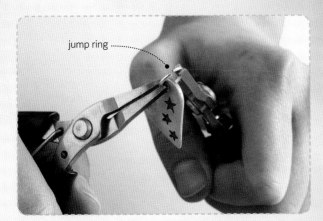

jump ring

14 **Once you are pleased** with the finish, attach the jump ring and chain. Using two pairs of pliers, gently twist the ends of the jump ring away from each other and thread one end through the hole in the charm. Twist the jump ring closed, then thread the finished pendant onto the chain.

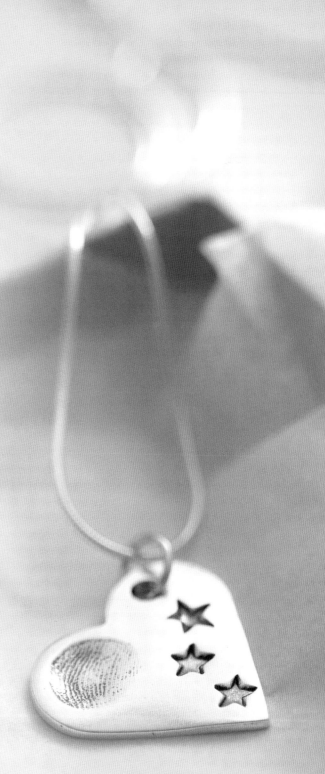

Two-toned nappy bag

Create this fabulous nappy bag in fabrics to suit your personal taste and style. If you'd like to make the bag more rigid, attach medium-weight fusible interfacing to all your fabric pieces before starting to sew them together.

YOU WILL NEED ✿ 127 x 81.5cm (50 x 32in) main fabric ✿ 89 x 117cm (35 x 46in) contrasting fabric for the lining ✿ ruler ✿ tailor's chalk or pencil ✿ scissors ✿ tracing paper ✿ marker pen ✿ pins ✿ sewing machine capable of zigzag stitch ✿ matching thread ✿ iron ✿ safety pin ✿ needle

1 **Measure and cut all the pieces** for the bag following the diagrams and instructions on page 249. Use tailor's chalk or pencil and a ruler to measure and mark all the pieces. If you need to cut two pieces of fabric from the same pattern piece, lay the fabric double and cut both at the same time.

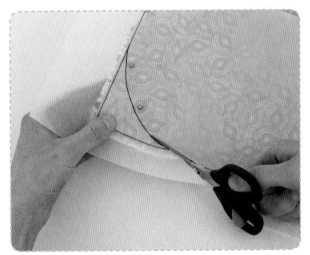

2 **Align the main and contrasting fabrics** for the back/flap on top of one another and pin together. Trace the template on page 249 onto the tracing paper, then line up the paper with the corner of the fabrics, as marked on the diagram. Pin the paper in place, then cut along the curved line to round off the corner. Repeat on the opposite corner.

3 **Fold the two inside pockets** right side to right side along the fold lines marked on the diagrams, then pin. Sew around the raw edges leaving a 1cm (½in) seam allowance. Leave a 7.5cm (3in) gap in the seam. Turn each pocket to the right side through the gap. Use a pin to pull out the corners (see step 5, p.192), then iron the pockets.

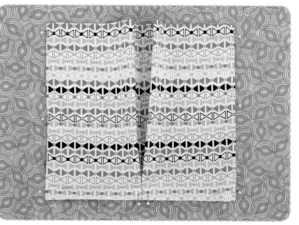

4 **Make a small box pleat** in the middle of each pocket, following the instructions on page 227. Pin each pocket in position as marked on the diagrams, right side up on the right side of the bag lining. Pin the smaller pocket to the lining of the bag front and the larger pocket to the lining of the bag back/flap.

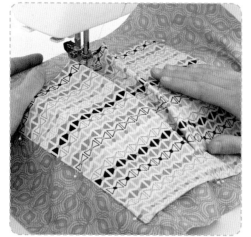

5 **Attach the pockets** to the lining by stitching along the middle stitch line of each box pleat, then around the bottom of each pocket and around the edges, leaving the top open. Each pocket now has two sections.

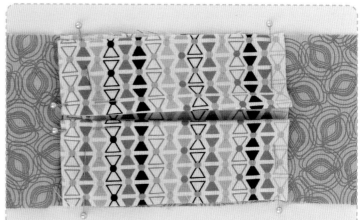

6 **Fold the two side pockets right side to right side** along the fold lines marked on the diagrams. Pin, then stitch the raw short edges together. Turn the pockets to the right side, then iron. Make a small box pleat in each pocket following steps 1–5 on page 227, then align the long edges of the pockets with the edges of one of the side/bottom strips, as shown. Pin, leaving the pockets open along one short edge. The openings should each be 11.5cm (4½in) from the corresponding end of the side/bottom strip. Attach the pockets by stitching around the sides and the bottom.

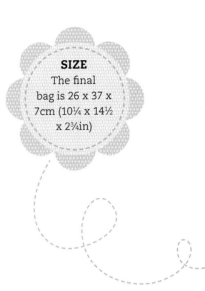

SIZE
The final
bag is 26 x 37 x
7cm (10¼ x 14½
x 2¾in)

7 **Pin the lining and main fabric** back/flap pieces together right side to right side. Leaving a 1cm (½in) seam allowance, stitch around the curved edge, between the two clip marks indicated on the diagrams.

8 **Clip into the seam allowance** at the clip marks, right up to the stitches. Trim the seam allowance to 3mm (⅛in), then clip around the curve. Turn to the right side and iron. The stitched, curved part is now the bag flap and the unstitched part is the bag back.

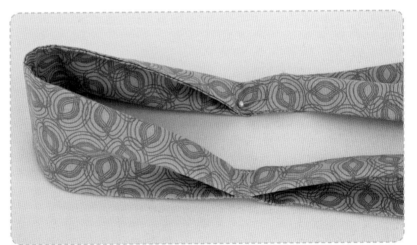

9 **Pin the lining and main fabric** front pieces together right side to right side. Stitch along the top edge only, then turn to the right side and iron.

10 **Make the strap by pinning the two strap pieces together,** right side to right side. Stitch together the long edges only, leaving the short edges unsewn. Turn the strap to the right side (see p.226) and iron. Find the centre of the strap and make two small pleats in the strap equidistant from the centre, as shown. Pin, then stitch through all the layers.

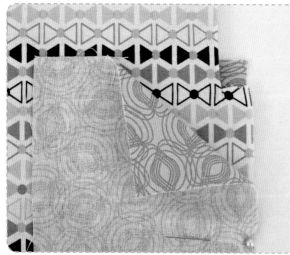

11 **Lay the two side/bottom strips** together, right side to right side, sandwiching the back of the bag between them. The side pockets should face the right side of the back of the bag. Pin together, leaving a 1cm (½in) seam allowance above the notch.

12 **Stitch through all three layers** to 1cm (½in) from the bottom edge of the back. With the bag still under the presser foot, snip at an angle 1cm (½in) into the side/bottom strips only. Do not snip through the back of the bag. The snip line is marked above in red, for reference.

13 **Turn the side/bottom strips** at the snips so their edges align with the bottom edge of the bag, then pin, as shown. Pivot the entire bag under the presser foot, then sew along the bottom edge to the next corner. Snip again as in step 12, turn the strips again, then pin them along the third side. Pivot the bag again, then sew along the third side.

14 **Stitch each end of the strap** right side to right side to each short edge of the side/bottom strip that you attached the side pockets to in step 6. Turn down the short edges of the other side/bottom strip by 1cm (½in) and iron. These will be finished by hand in step 17.

15 **Pin, then stitch together** the long raw edges of both side/bottom strips, with their wrong sides together.

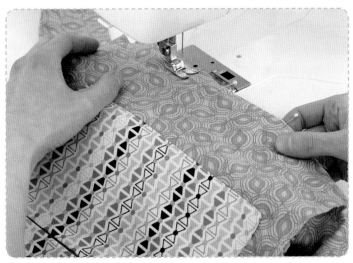

16 **Pin the front of the bag** to the sewn-up raw edges of the side/bottom strip, right side to right side. Stitch, snipping and pivoting at the corners as in step 12. Trim the seam allowances to 5mm (¼in), then zigzag them to neaten.

17 **Working on the inside of the bag,** hand-stitch to the strap the turned-down edge that you made in step 14. This will close the hole. Turn the bag to the right side and iron.

TOP TIP *Make sure the strap is not twisted before you attach it in step 14.*

Tiny footprints plaque

There's nothing cuter than a pair of tiny feet. This project can be done at any age, even when your baby is very small. You may find it easier to get an impression while your baby is lying down, with the plate tilted almost completely vertical, otherwise you will need someone to hold baby for you.

YOU WILL NEED ❀ extra-light, white, air-dry clay ❀ rolling pin ❀ round bowl, at least 14cm (5½in) ❀ knife ❀ plate or other firm, portable surface ❀ drinking straw ❀ 70–100cm (27½–40in) ribbon

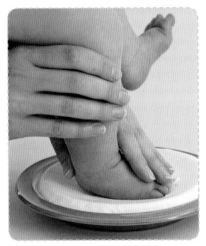

1 **Remove the clay from** its package and place it on a clean, flat work surface. Using the rolling pin, roll the clay out so that it is approximately 5mm (¼in) thick.

2 **Place the bowl lightly** on the clay and cut around it with a knife to make a perfect circle. Remove the excess clay and lift the bowl off. Put the clay circle on a plate or other firm, portable surface.

3 **Gently push** your baby's feet into the clay, one at a time. Be sure to get an imprint of each toe and make sure that the feet imprints are even and level. If you fail to get a clear imprint, re-roll the clay and start again.

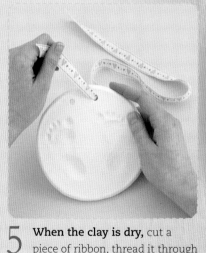

push the
straw
through
the clay

4 **Once you have** a clear imprint,
put the clay back on the clean,
flat work surface. Make two
holes in the top of the plaque
with the drinking straw. Ensure
the holes are level and centred.
Leave the clay to dry.

5 **When the clay is dry,** cut a
piece of ribbon, thread it through
the holes to make a loop and
finish with a bow. Your plaque is
now ready to hang on the wall.

Baby gift cards

A handmade gift card is a little work of art that the recipient will treasure for years to come. Choose scrapbook papers in patterns and colours to suit your creations. Use the templates provided or create your own unique designs using the same technique.

YOU WILL NEED ❀ shop-bought envelope in the size and colour of your choice ❀ heavyweight coloured card ❀ craft knife or scissors ❀ ruler ❀ cutting mat (optional) ❀ an assortment of scrapbook papers ❀ glue stick ❀ pencil ❀ tracing paper

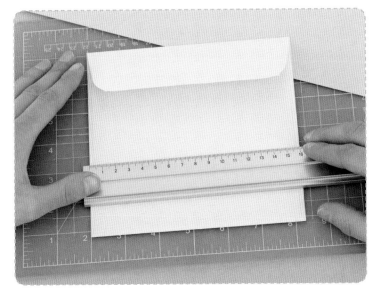

Fold the card in half along the score line

1 **Measure the shop-bought envelope,** then cut the card so that the finished card will fit inside the envelope. This means that when the card is folded, it is approximately 5mm (¼in) smaller than the envelope in both height and width.

2 **Use a ruler and the blunt side** of the craft knife or the scissors blade to carefully score the card along the fold line. Take care not to cut through the card. Fold the card along the score line.

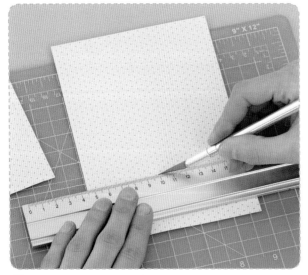

3 **Measure the front of the card,** then cut a piece of scrapbook paper 1.5cm (½in) smaller on all four sides than the folded card. This will leave a margin all around the paper once it is in position.

4 **Stick the piece of scrapbook paper** to the front of the folded card using a glue stick. Make sure the paper is centred and square with the edges of the card.

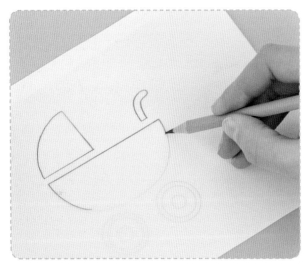

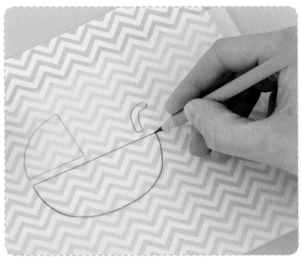

5 **Using a pencil,** trace your choice of template from page 242 onto the tracing paper. Turn the tracing paper over and pencil over the traced lines.

6 **Turn the tracing paper over again** so the image is the right way round, then lay the tracing paper on the scrapbook paper. Pencil over the traced lines yet again to transfer the image to the paper. Use different scrapbook paper for each part of the design.

7 **Once you have transferred** the different parts of the design to the different pieces of scrapbook paper, cut the shapes out using the craft knife or scissors.

8 **Before you glue anything in place,** lay the main parts of the design on the printed paper to check their positioning.

9 **Once you are happy with** the positioning, use the glue stick to glue the main parts of the design in place.

10 **Finish by gluing the smaller details** in place, then leave the card to dry.

Cupcake
gift set

If you need a present for a new mum, this cupcake gift set is cute and easy to make. The instructions are for four cupcakes but simply adjust the quantities if you'd like to make more.

YOU WILL NEED ✿ four baby vests size 0–3 months in assorted colours
✿ one pair of scratch mitts ✿ one pair of socks ✿ one cake box approximately
16 x 16cm (6½ x 6½in) (optional) ✿ decorative-edge scissors (optional)
✿ plain or patterned paper, or four jumbo-sized cupcake cases
✿ 2m (79in) ribbon ✿ clear tape ✿ scissors

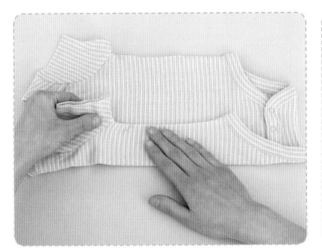

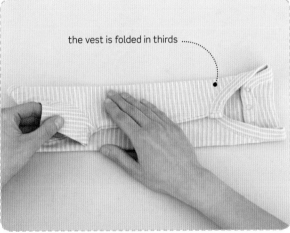

the vest is folded in thirds

1 **Place one baby vest** face up on a flat surface. Fold the sleeve and about one-third of the side of the vest in towards the middle of the vest, as shown.

2 **Fold the opposite sleeve** and side in towards the middle by an equal amount, as shown.

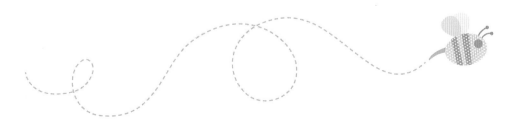

TOP TIP *Choose clothing in a variety of colours that remind you of delicious icing.*

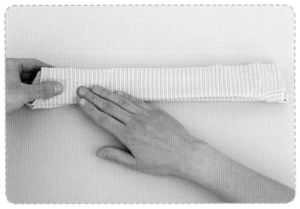

3 **Now fold the vest in half.** You should have a strip approximately 5cm (2in) wide.

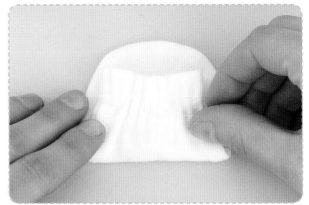

4 **Fold one scratch mitt or sock** so its upper edge comes about three-quarters of the way up the folded piece.

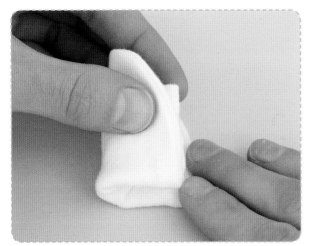

5 **Now fold the mitt or sock** in half widthways and hold it in place so the folds do not come undone.

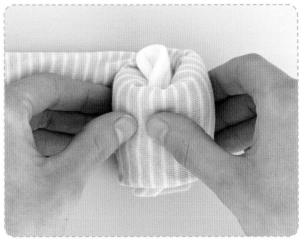

6 **Place the folded mitt or sock** on one end of the folded vest strip, with its top sticking out slightly. Start rolling the vest up around the mitt or sock to form the cupcake shape.

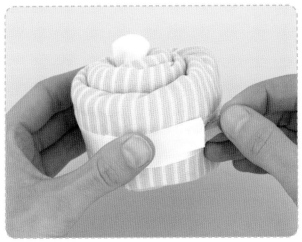

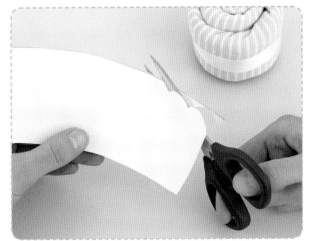

7 **Holding everything securely,** wrap a piece of ribbon around the cupcake and secure it with clear tape to hold it all together. Repeat steps 1–7 to make three more cupcakes.

8 **Trace the cupcake case template** on page 236 onto plain or patterned paper and cut out four. Use decorative-edge or normal scissors to make a fancy edge on the curved side of each piece of paper. Alternatively, use bought jumbo-sized cupcake cases.

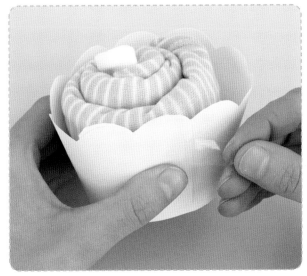

9 **Wrap the paper cupcake case** around the cupcake and secure it in place with clear tape.

10 **Arrange the cupcakes in the cake box** or arrange them creatively on a plate or decorative cake stand. Tie a ribbon around the box to keep it closed, then present it to mum.

First birthday
silhouette

To capture a clear profile of your baby, he must be able to hold his head up, so why not make this charming silhouette as a first birthday keepsake? You could even start a birthday tradition, making a new silhouette each year so you can look back and see how your baby has changed.

YOU WILL NEED ✿ craft knife ✿ ruler ✿ cutting mat ✿ patterned paper, large enough to fit the frame
✿ photo of your baby's profile, enlarged to the size of your choice ✿ tracing paper ✿ pencil
✿ scissors ✿ coordinating plain paper, large enough for the silhouette ✿ low-tack tape
✿ glue stick or spray mount ✿ 15 x 15cm (6 x 6in) frame, or the size of your choice

 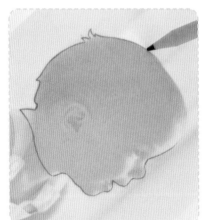 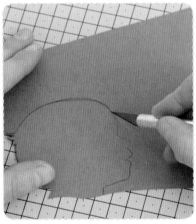

1 **Using a craft knife,** ruler, and cutting mat, cut the patterned paper to fit your frame.

2 **Trace your baby's profile** from the photo onto the tracing paper, then cut it out with scissors. This will be your template.

3 **Lightly attach the template** to the plain paper with low-tack tape. Trace around the template with a pencil, then carefully cut the silhouette out with a craft knife.

 Apply glue or spray mount to the back of the silhouette, then centre it on the patterned paper and smooth it down. Once the adhesive is dry, place the finished silhouette in the frame.

Sea-side stencilled vests

see pages 174-177

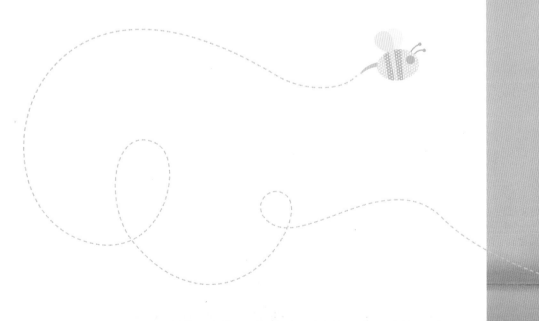

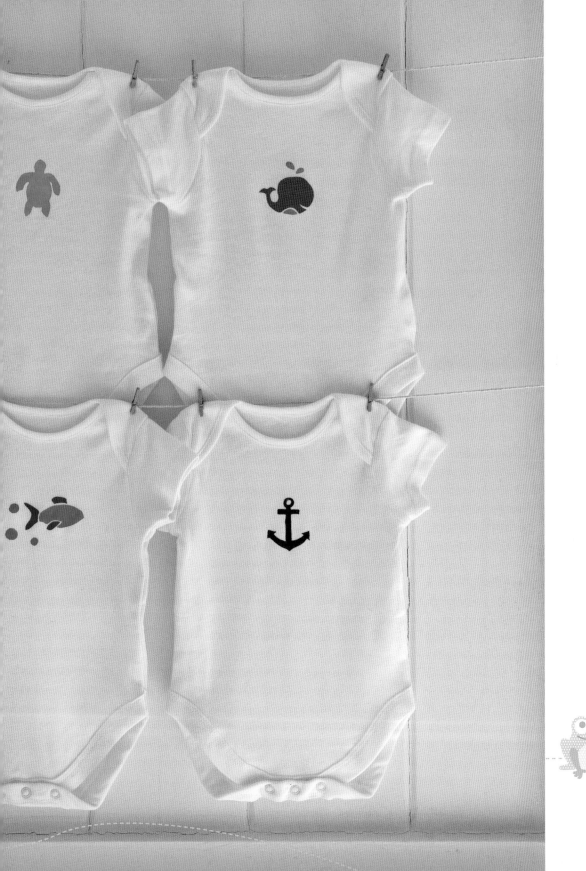

How to hand-stitch and embroider

Use this selection of common embroidery and hand stitches to decorate your projects. A small embroidery motif on a toy, blanket, or piece of clothing can set it apart as something lovingly crafted and to be cherished for years. Always secure your stitches at the back of the work or with the thread tails hidden beneath satin stitch.

Running stitch

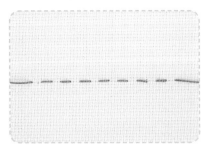

Work the needle and thread in and out of the fabric, creating stitches of even length that are evenly spaced.

Blanket stitch

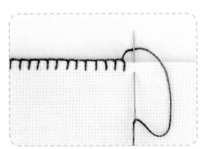

Working from left to right, insert the needle through the right side of the fabric. As the needle appears at the edge, wrap the thread under the needle and pull the needle through.

Satin stitch

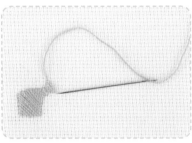

Bring the needle to the front at one side of the shape to be worked. Take it over the shape and to the back on the opposite side. Continue using long, smooth stitches without pulling, as this would pucker the fabric.

French knot

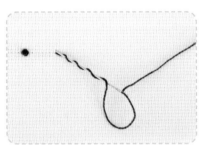

Bring the needle to the front of the fabric. Wrap the thread around the needle, then push the needle to the back, just next to the hole where it emerged from the back.

Flat fell stitch

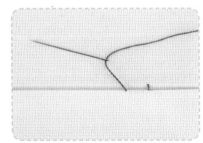

1 **Great for seaming** two overlapping layers on a project, particularly the raw edge of a non-fraying fabric such as felt. Working from right to left, take the needle to the front through both layers of fabric.

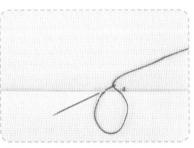

2 **Reinsert the needle** through the first layer of fabric only, just above where the thread came out, and then bring it back out, one stitch along, through both layers of fabric.

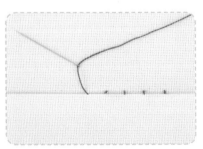

3 **Continue working,** taking care not to pull the thread too tight. You will have tiny stitches on the right side and longer stitches on the wrong side.

Back stitch

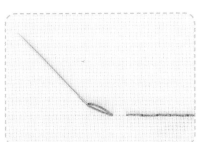

1 **Take the needle** to the back of the fabric, take a stitch forwards, then bring the needle back out.

2 **Take a stitch backwards,** inserting the needle in the end of the last stitch.

3 **Continue making stitches** forwards underneath the fabric and backwards on top.

Chain stitch

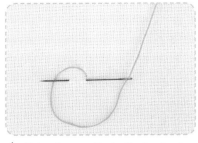

1 **Take the needle to the back** of the fabric, take a stitch forwards and bring the needle back out, looping the thread over the point of the needle as it emerges.

2 **Pull the needle** through the loop, then take it to the back of the fabric again, inserting it where it came out in step 1.

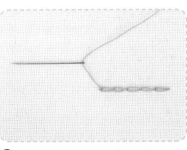

3 **Repeat steps 1 and 2** to form a chain of loops. Try to keep the loops all the same size so that the chain looks even and neat.

Lazy daisy stitch

1 **To make the first petal,** take the needle to the back of the fabric, make a stitch, and bring the needle back out, looping the thread over the point of the needle as it emerges.

2 **Pull the needle through** the loop then make a short stitch to the back of the fabric to secure the petal in place.

3 **Make the next** and subsequent petals in the same way, starting each one at the centre of the daisy and working around.

How to make a fabric tube

1 **Having sewn the two** long edges of the fabric together, right side to right side, attach a safety pin to one of the short ends.

2 **Push the safety pin** into the opening at the end. It will pull the end of the tube with it.

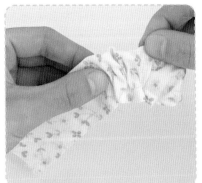

3 **Using both hands,** work the safety pin through the tube. The fabric will bunch up as you go, but keep hold of the pin and continue pushing it through.

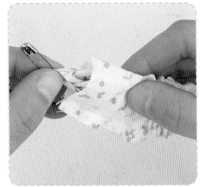

4 **Work the pin completely** through the tube until it comes out at the other end.

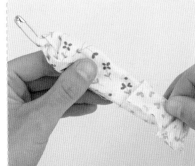

5 **Pull on the safety pin** and the rest of the tube will follow. The fabric tube will now be the right way out.

6 **Iron the tube flat,** positioning the seam either to one side or in the middle, depending on the project.

How to make box pleats for the projects

1 **Referring to the pattern** for your project, fold and stitch your pocket as required. Working along the bottom edge of the pocket strip, take one colour of tailor's chalk and measure and lightly mark your fold lines along this edge.

2 **Using a second colour of chalk,** measure and lightly mark your stitch lines according to the pattern or instructions.

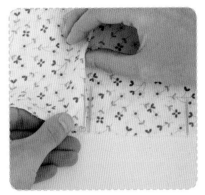

3 **Fold the fabric** up on one fold line to meet the central stitch line, creating a pleat. Pin the pleat in place.

4 **Fold the next fold line up** and back to meet the same stitch line, creating a second pleat.

5 **Pin the second pleat in place,** creating a box pleat. Do not overlap the two folded edges, but ensure they sit right against one another. Repeat steps 1–5 for any other pleats on the pocket strip, if necessary.

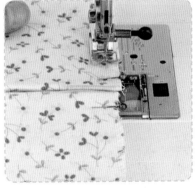

6 **Using a straight stitch,** sew along the bottom, stitching the pleats in place. Remove the pins as you work. Iron the pocket strip.

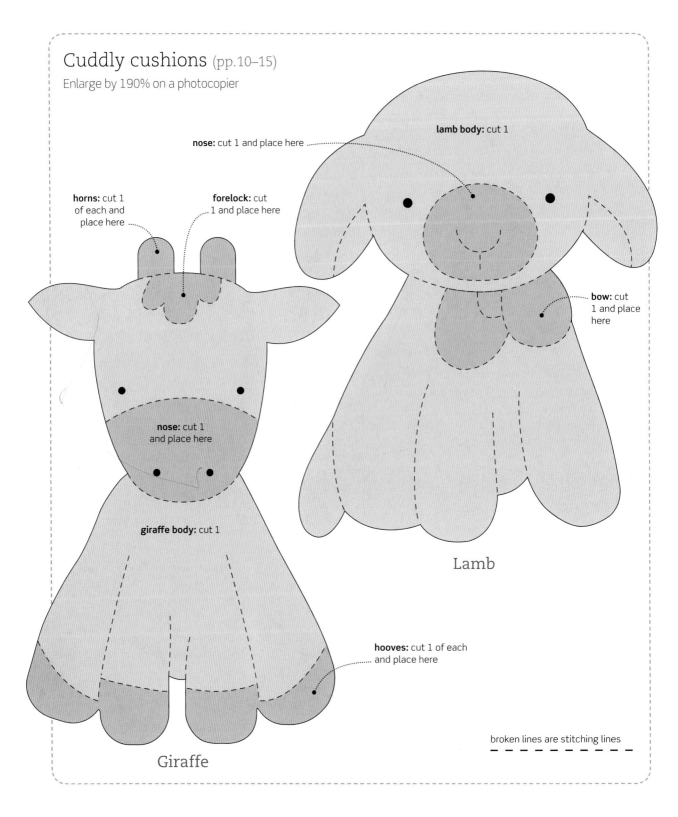

Cuddly cushions (pp.10–15)
Enlarge by 190% on a photocopier

nose: cut 1 and place here

lamb body: cut 1

horns: cut 1 of each and place here

forelock: cut 1 and place here

bow: cut 1 and place here

nose: cut 1 and place here

giraffe body: cut 1

Lamb

hooves: cut 1 of each and place here

Giraffe

broken lines are stitching lines

Counting sheep blanket (pp.36–39)

Enlarge by 190% on a photocopier

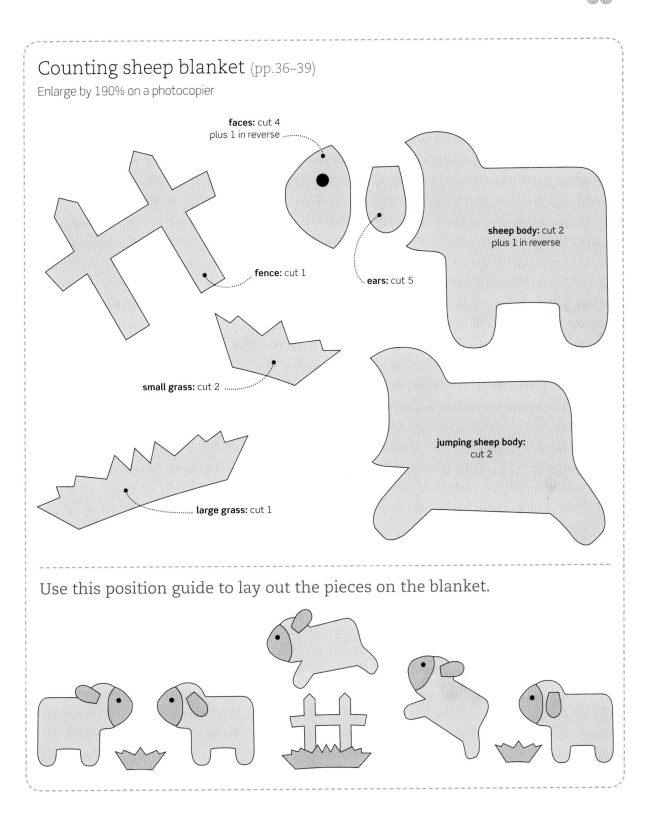

faces: cut 4
plus 1 in reverse

fence: cut 1

ears: cut 5

sheep body: cut 2
plus 1 in reverse

small grass: cut 2

large grass: cut 1

jumping sheep body:
cut 2

Use this position guide to lay out the pieces on the blanket.

Felt friends mobile (pp.56–59)
Enlarge by 180% on a photocopier

Donkey

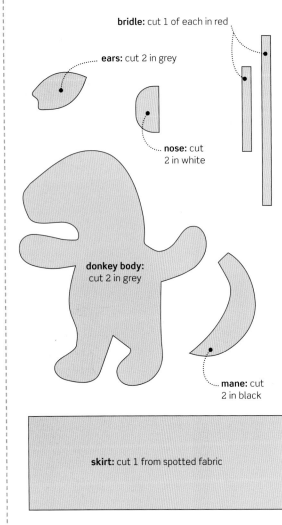

bridle: cut 1 of each in red

ears: cut 2 in grey

nose: cut 2 in white

donkey body: cut 2 in grey

mane: cut 2 in black

skirt: cut 1 from spotted fabric

Squirrel

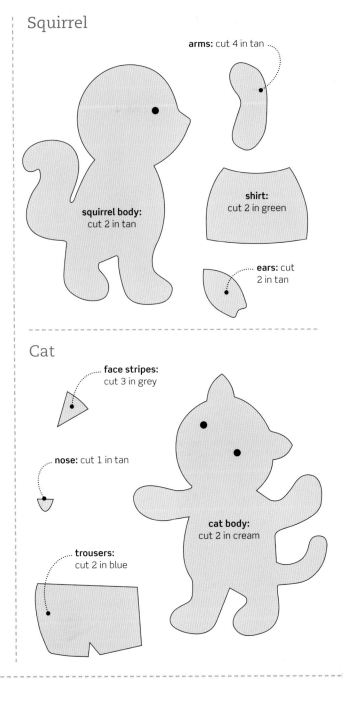

arms: cut 4 in tan

squirrel body: cut 2 in tan

shirt: cut 2 in green

ears: cut 2 in tan

Cat

face stripes: cut 3 in grey

nose: cut 1 in tan

cat body: cut 2 in cream

trousers: cut 2 in blue

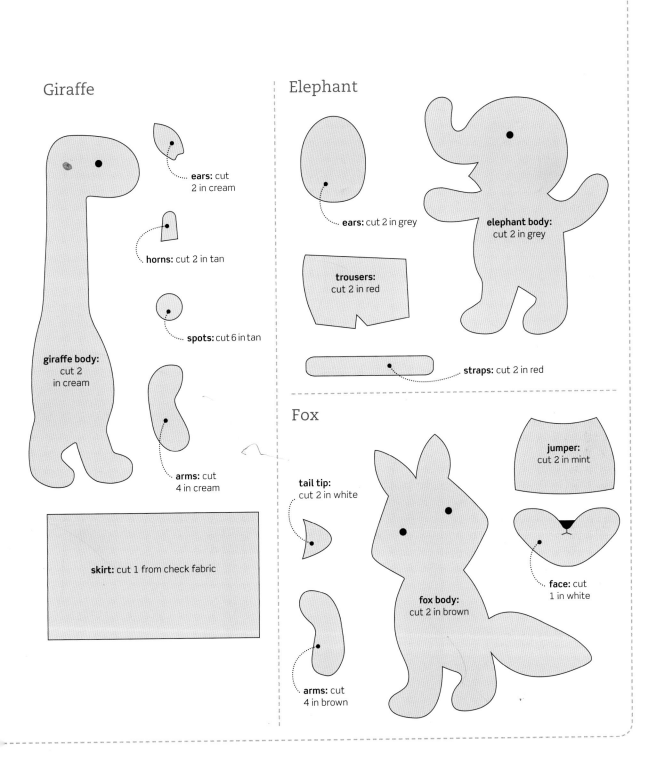

Giraffe

ears: cut 2 in cream

horns: cut 2 in tan

spots: cut 6 in tan

giraffe body: cut 2 in cream

arms: cut 4 in cream

skirt: cut 1 from check fabric

Elephant

ears: cut 2 in grey

trousers: cut 2 in red

elephant body: cut 2 in grey

straps: cut 2 in red

Fox

tail tip: cut 2 in white

arms: cut 4 in brown

fox body: cut 2 in brown

jumper: cut 2 in mint

face: cut 1 in white

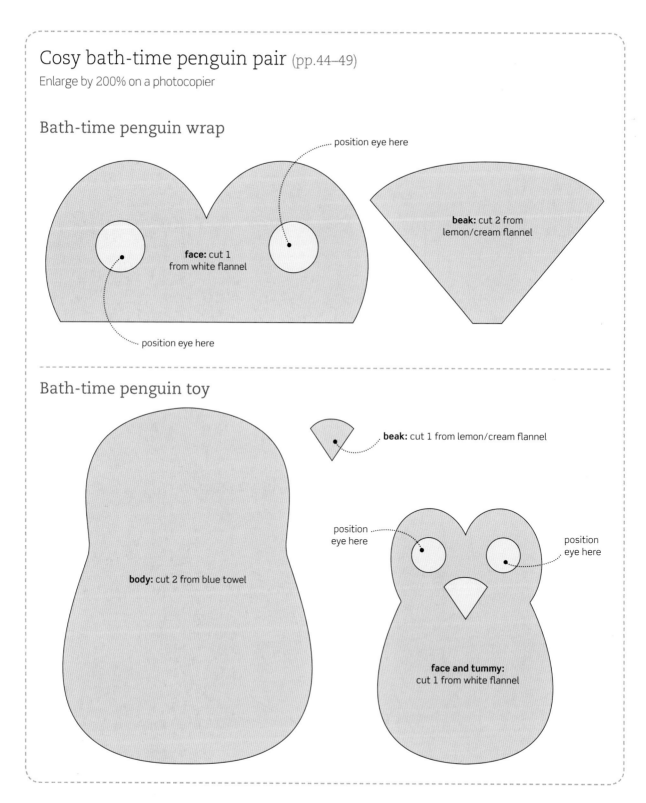

Cosy bath-time penguin pair (pp.44–49)

Enlarge by 200% on a photocopier

Bath-time penguin wrap

position eye here

face: cut 1
from white flannel

beak: cut 2 from
lemon/cream flannel

position eye here

Bath-time penguin toy

beak: cut 1 from lemon/cream flannel

position
eye here

position
eye here

body: cut 2 from blue towel

face and tummy:
cut 1 from white flannel

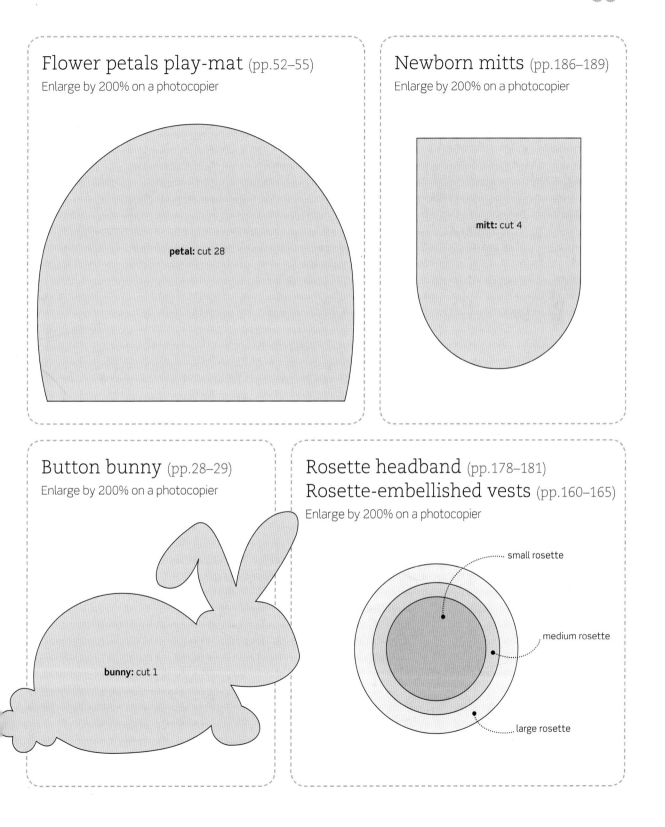

Flower petals play-mat (pp.52–55)
Enlarge by 200% on a photocopier

petal: cut 28

Newborn mitts (pp.186–189)
Enlarge by 200% on a photocopier

mitt: cut 4

Button bunny (pp.28–29)
Enlarge by 200% on a photocopier

bunny: cut 1

Rosette headband (pp.178–181)
Rosette-embellished vests (pp.160–165)
Enlarge by 200% on a photocopier

small rosette

medium rosette

large rosette

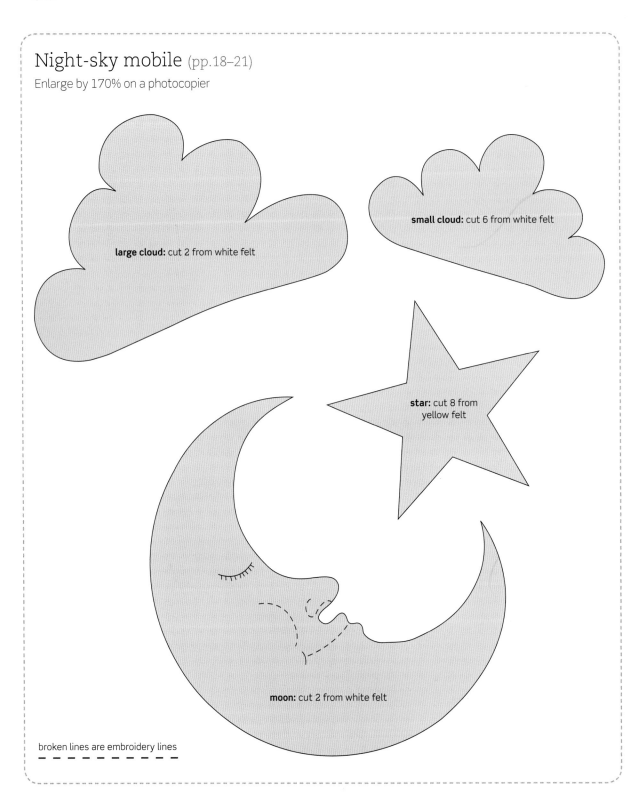

Night-sky mobile (pp.18–21)

Enlarge by 170% on a photocopier

large cloud: cut 2 from white felt

small cloud: cut 6 from white felt

star: cut 8 from yellow felt

moon: cut 2 from white felt

broken lines are embroidery lines

Summertime booties (pp.154–159)

Enlarge by 140% on a photocopier

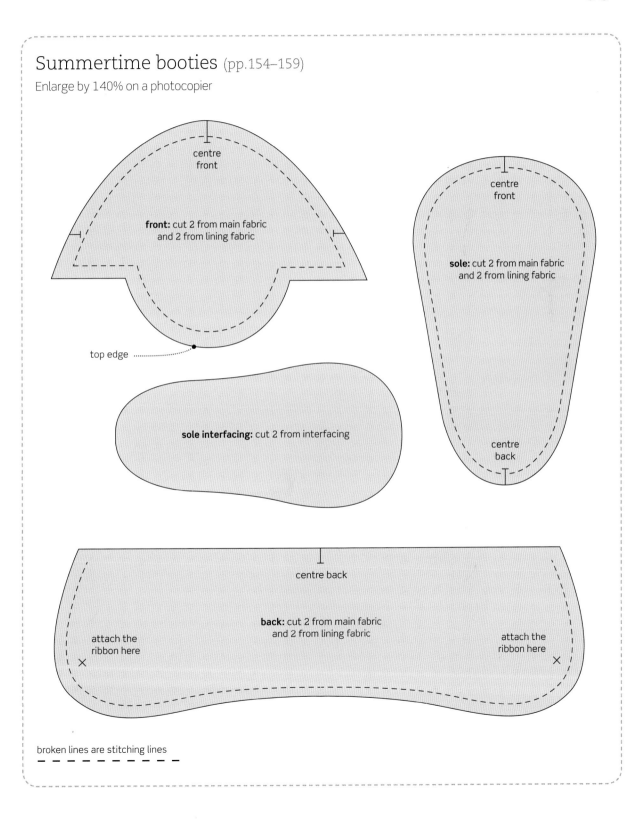

centre
front

front: cut 2 from main fabric
and 2 from lining fabric

top edge ·····

centre
front

sole: cut 2 from main fabric
and 2 from lining fabric

centre
back

sole interfacing: cut 2 from interfacing

centre back

back: cut 2 from main fabric
and 2 from lining fabric

attach the
ribbon here

attach the
ribbon here

broken lines are stitching lines

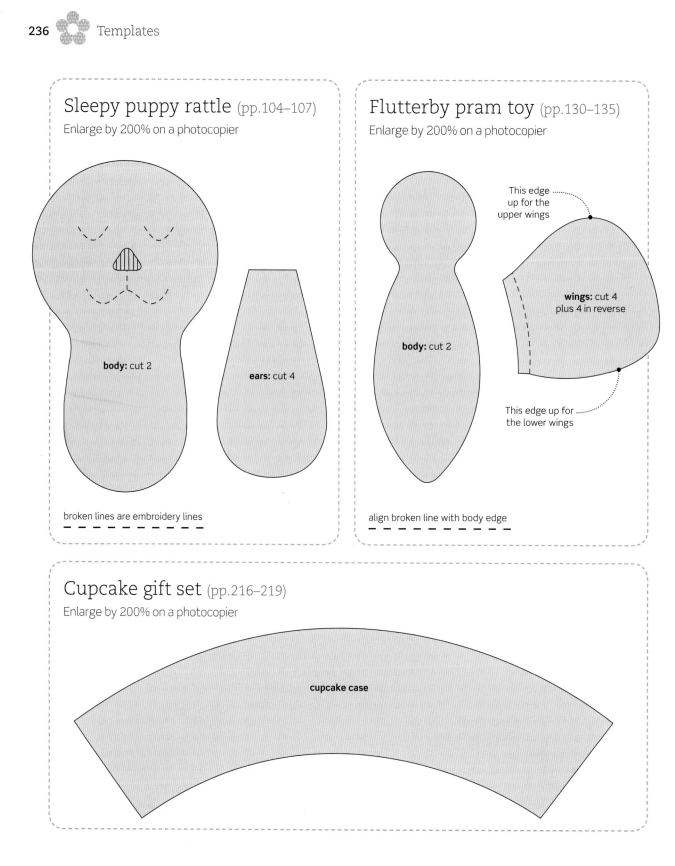

Sleepy puppy rattle (pp.104–107)
Enlarge by 200% on a photocopier

body: cut 2

ears: cut 4

broken lines are embroidery lines

Flutterby pram toy (pp.130–135)
Enlarge by 200% on a photocopier

This edge up for the upper wings

body: cut 2

wings: cut 4 plus 4 in reverse

This edge up for the lower wings

align broken line with body edge

Cupcake gift set (pp.216–219)
Enlarge by 200% on a photocopier

cupcake case

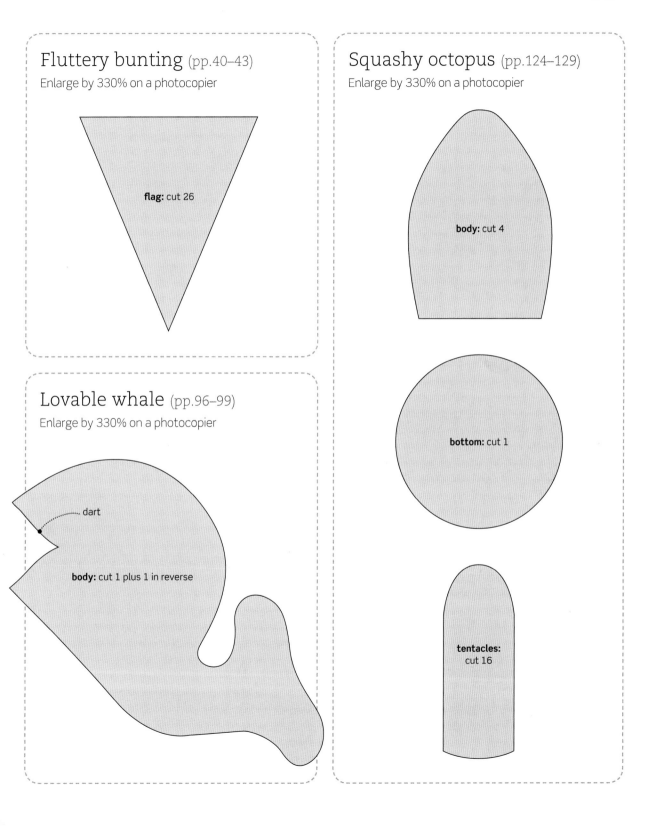

Fluttery bunting (pp.40–43)

Enlarge by 330% on a photocopier

flag: cut 26

Lovable whale (pp.96–99)

Enlarge by 330% on a photocopier

········ dart

body: cut 1 plus 1 in reverse

Squashy octopus (pp.124–129)

Enlarge by 330% on a photocopier

body: cut 4

bottom: cut 1

tentacles: cut 16

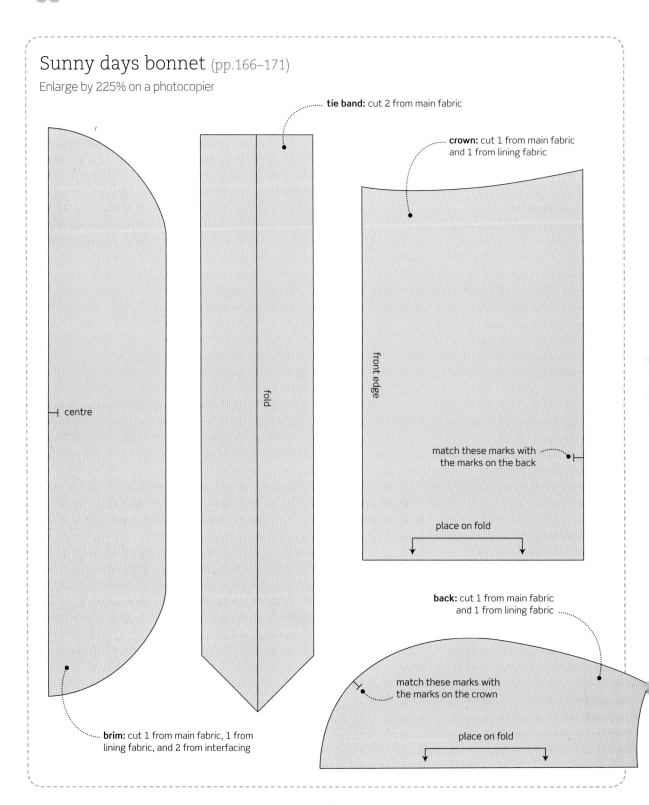

Sunny days bonnet (pp.166–171)

Enlarge by 225% on a photocopier

tie band: cut 2 from main fabric

crown: cut 1 from main fabric and 1 from lining fabric

centre

fold

front edge

match these marks with the marks on the back

place on fold

back: cut 1 from main fabric and 1 from lining fabric

match these marks with the marks on the crown

place on fold

brim: cut 1 from main fabric, 1 from lining fabric, and 2 from interfacing

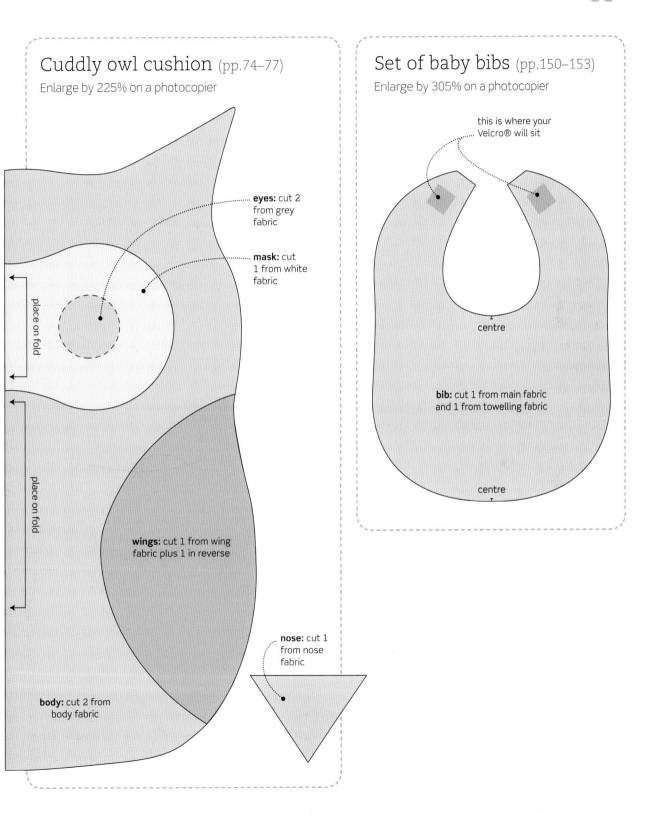

Cuddly owl cushion (pp.74–77)

Enlarge by 225% on a photocopier

eyes: cut 2 from grey fabric

mask: cut 1 from white fabric

place on fold

place on fold

wings: cut 1 from wing fabric plus 1 in reverse

nose: cut 1 from nose fabric

body: cut 2 from body fabric

Set of baby bibs (pp.150–153)

Enlarge by 305% on a photocopier

this is where your Velcro® will sit

centre

bib: cut 1 from main fabric and 1 from towelling fabric

centre

Simple summer dress (pp.190–195)

Enlarge by 400% on a photocopier

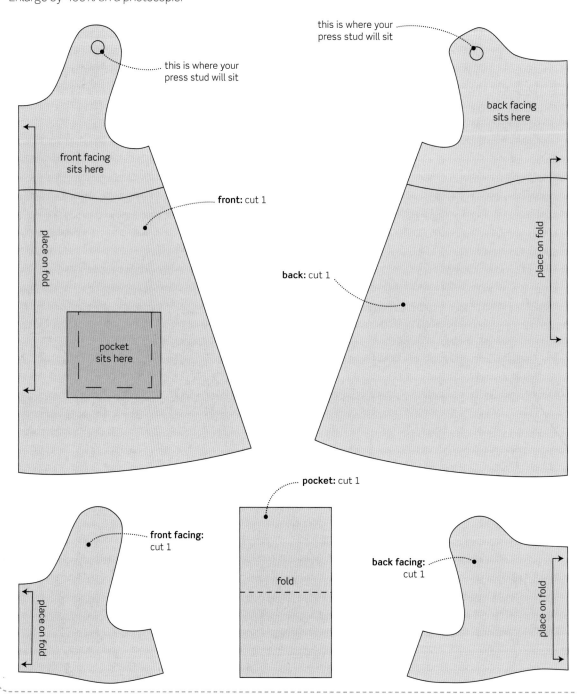

this is where your press stud will sit

this is where your press stud will sit

front facing sits here

back facing sits here

front: cut 1

back: cut 1

place on fold

place on fold

pocket sits here

pocket: cut 1

front facing: cut 1

fold

back facing: cut 1

place on fold

place on fold

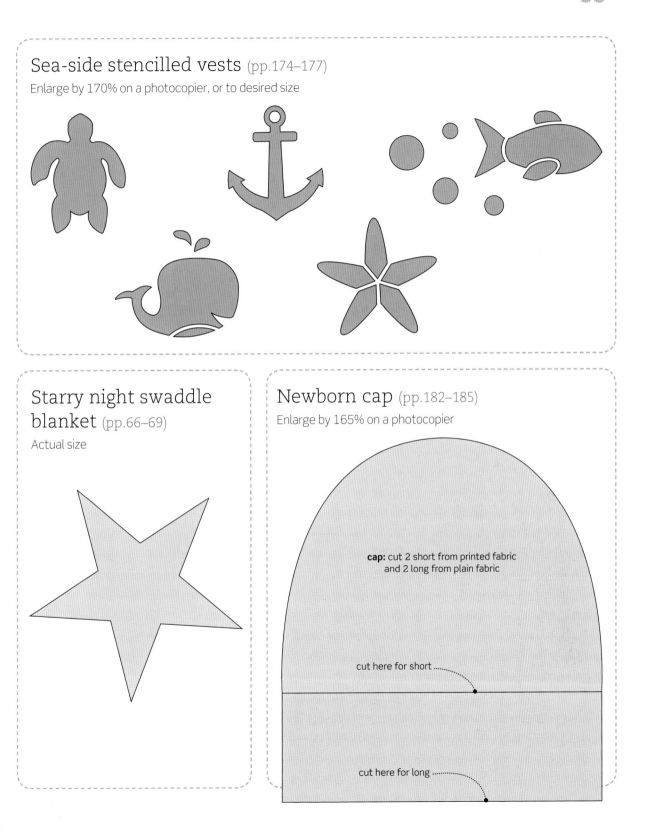

Sea-side stencilled vests (pp.174–177)

Enlarge by 170% on a photocopier, or to desired size

Starry night swaddle blanket (pp.66–69)

Actual size

Newborn cap (pp.182–185)

Enlarge by 165% on a photocopier

cap: cut 2 short from printed fabric
and 2 long from plain fabric

cut here for short ....

cut here for long ....

Baby gift cards (pp.212–215)

Enlarge by 155% on a photocopier

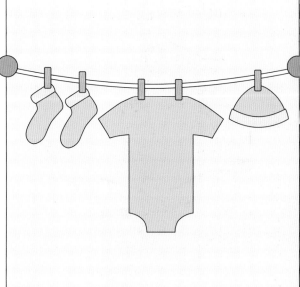

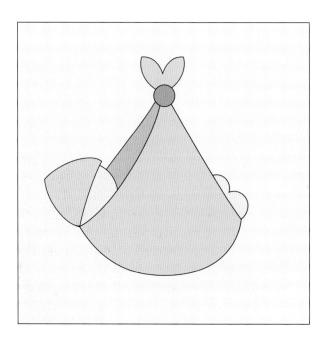

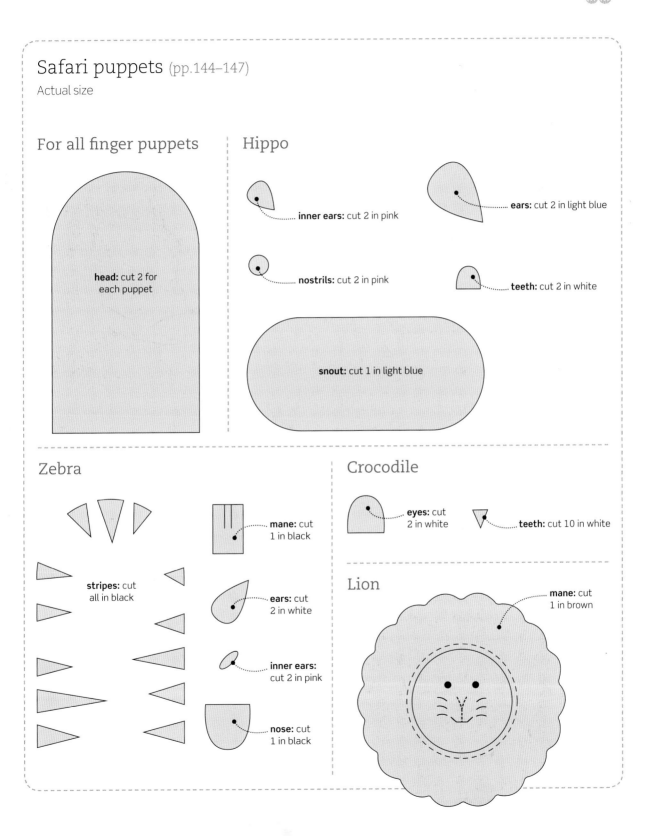

Safari puppets (pp.144–147)

Actual size

For all finger puppets

head: cut 2 for each puppet

Hippo

inner ears: cut 2 in pink

ears: cut 2 in light blue

nostrils: cut 2 in pink

teeth: cut 2 in white

snout: cut 1 in light blue

Zebra

stripes: cut all in black

mane: cut 1 in black

ears: cut 2 in white

inner ears: cut 2 in pink

nose: cut 1 in black

Crocodile

eyes: cut 2 in white

teeth: cut 10 in white

Lion

mane: cut 1 in brown

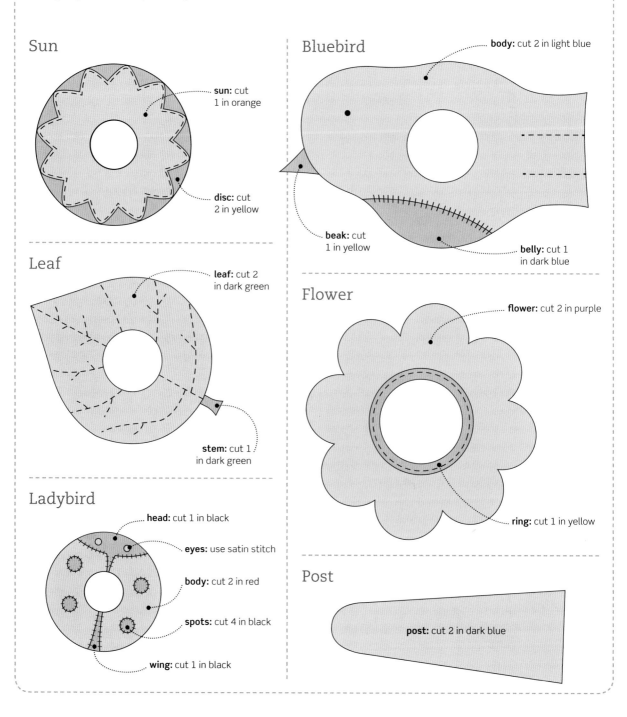

Nature-themed stacking rings (pp.112–115)
Enlarge by 145% on a photocopier

Sun

sun: cut 1 in orange

disc: cut 2 in yellow

Leaf

leaf: cut 2 in dark green

stem: cut 1 in dark green

Ladybird

head: cut 1 in black

eyes: use satin stitch

body: cut 2 in red

spots: cut 4 in black

wing: cut 1 in black

Bluebird

body: cut 2 in light blue

beak: cut 1 in yellow

belly: cut 1 in dark blue

Flower

flower: cut 2 in purple

ring: cut 1 in yellow

Post

post: cut 2 in dark blue

Floppy mouse toy (pp.136–143)

Enlarge by 225% on a photocopier

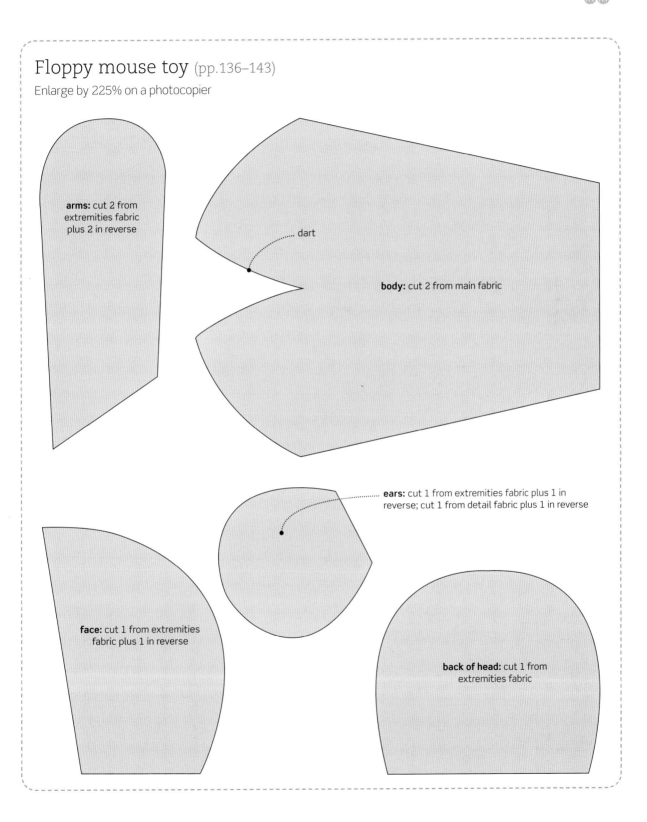

arms: cut 2 from extremities fabric plus 2 in reverse

dart

body: cut 2 from main fabric

ears: cut 1 from extremities fabric plus 1 in reverse; cut 1 from detail fabric plus 1 in reverse

face: cut 1 from extremities fabric plus 1 in reverse

back of head: cut 1 from extremities fabric

Fairy tale house doorstop (pp.60–65)

Enlarge on a photocopier to fit your juice carton, approximately 170%

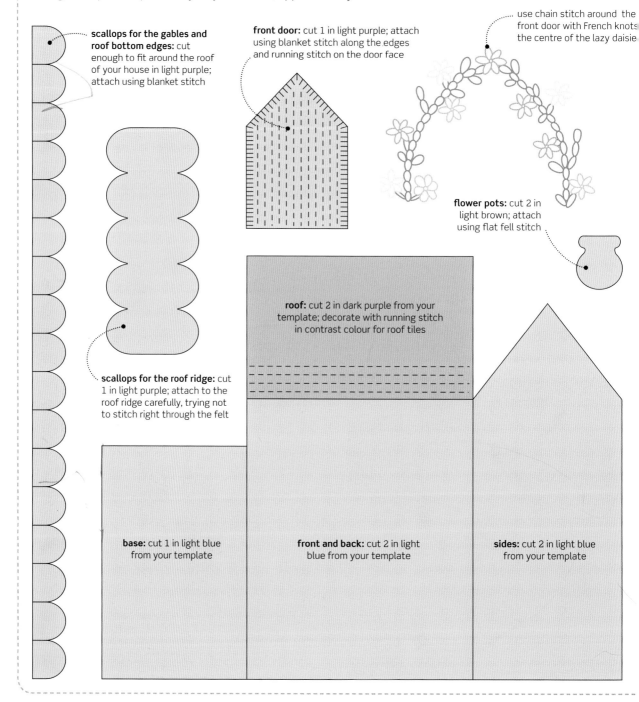

scallops for the gables and roof bottom edges: cut enough to fit around the roof of your house in light purple; attach using blanket stitch

front door: cut 1 in light purple; attach using blanket stitch along the edges and running stitch on the door face

use chain stitch around the front door with French knots the centre of the lazy daisie

flower pots: cut 2 in light brown; attach using flat fell stitch

roof: cut 2 in dark purple from your template; decorate with running stitch in contrast colour for roof tiles

scallops for the roof ridge: cut 1 in light purple; attach to the roof ridge carefully, trying not to stitch right through the felt

base: cut 1 in light blue from your template

front and back: cut 2 in light blue from your template

sides: cut 2 in light blue from your template

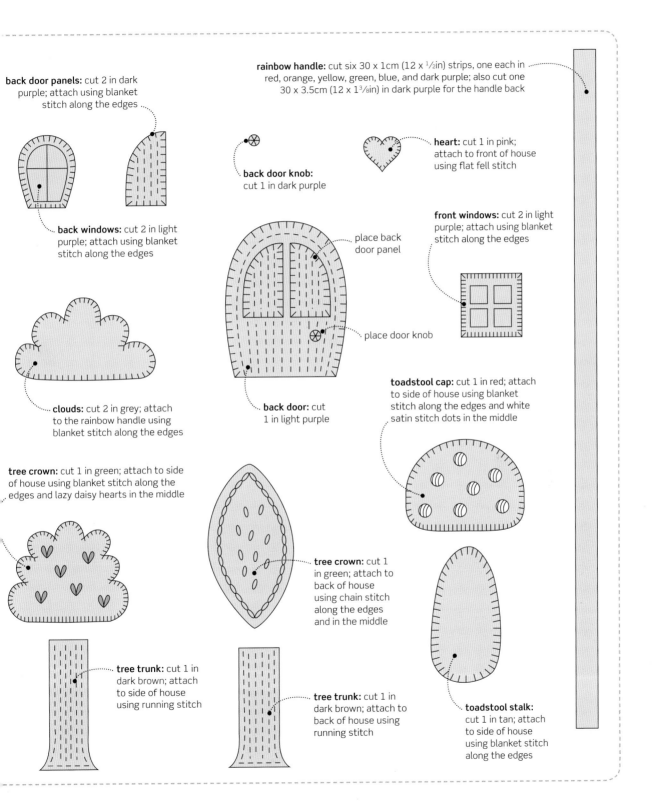

back door panels: cut 2 in dark purple; attach using blanket stitch along the edges

back windows: cut 2 in light purple; attach using blanket stitch along the edges

rainbow handle: cut six 30 x 1cm (12 x ½in) strips, one each in red, orange, yellow, green, blue, and dark purple; also cut one 30 x 3.5cm (12 x 1⅜in) in dark purple for the handle back

back door knob: cut 1 in dark purple

heart: cut 1 in pink; attach to front of house using flat fell stitch

front windows: cut 2 in light purple; attach using blanket stitch along the edges

place back door panel

place door knob

clouds: cut 2 in grey; attach to the rainbow handle using blanket stitch along the edges

back door: cut 1 in light purple

toadstool cap: cut 1 in red; attach to side of house using blanket stitch along the edges and white satin stitch dots in the middle

tree crown: cut 1 in green; attach to side of house using blanket stitch along the edges and lazy daisy hearts in the middle

tree crown: cut 1 in green; attach to back of house using chain stitch along the edges and in the middle

tree trunk: cut 1 in dark brown; attach to side of house using running stitch

tree trunk: cut 1 in dark brown; attach to back of house using running stitch

toadstool stalk: cut 1 in tan; attach to side of house using blanket stitch along the edges

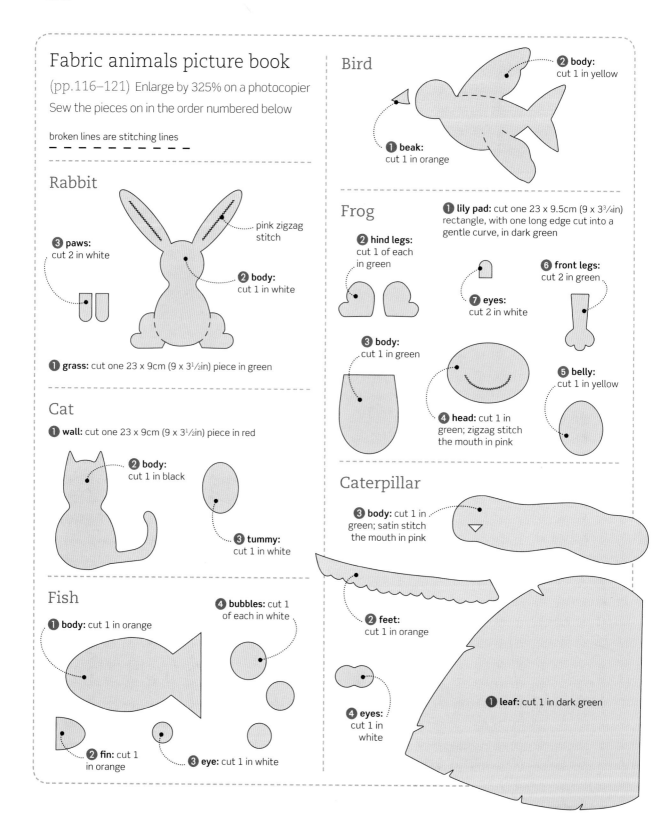

Fabric animals picture book

(pp.116–121) Enlarge by 325% on a photocopier

Sew the pieces on in the order numbered below

broken lines are stitching lines
▬ ▬ ▬ ▬ ▬ ▬ ▬ ▬ ▬

Rabbit

pink zigzag stitch

3 paws: cut 2 in white

2 body: cut 1 in white

1 grass: cut one 23 x 9cm (9 x 3½in) piece in green

Cat

1 wall: cut one 23 x 9cm (9 x 3½in) piece in red

2 body: cut 1 in black

3 tummy: cut 1 in white

Fish

1 body: cut 1 in orange

4 bubbles: cut 1 of each in white

2 fin: cut 1 in orange

3 eye: cut 1 in white

Bird

2 body: cut 1 in yellow

1 beak: cut 1 in orange

Frog

1 lily pad: cut one 23 x 9.5cm (9 x 3¾in) rectangle, with one long edge cut into a gentle curve, in dark green

2 hind legs: cut 1 of each in green

6 front legs: cut 2 in green

7 eyes: cut 2 in white

3 body: cut 1 in green

5 belly: cut 1 in yellow

4 head: cut 1 in green; zigzag stitch the mouth in pink

Caterpillar

3 body: cut 1 in green; satin stitch the mouth in pink

2 feet: cut 1 in orange

4 eyes: cut 1 in white

1 leaf: cut 1 in dark green

Two-toned nappy bag (pp.204–209)

Cut all fabric pieces to size according to the diagrams

Enlarge the rounded flap corner template by 265%

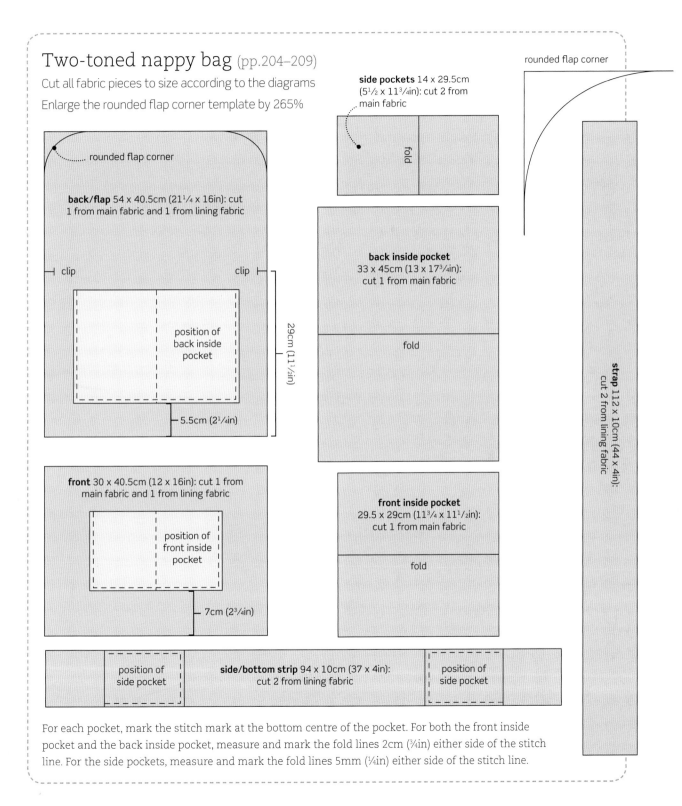

rounded flap corner

side pockets 14 x 29.5cm (5½ x 11¾in): cut 2 from main fabric

fold

rounded flap corner

back/flap 54 x 40.5cm (21¼ x 16in): cut 1 from main fabric and 1 from lining fabric

clip

clip

position of back inside pocket

29cm (11½in)

5.5cm (2¼in)

back inside pocket 33 x 45cm (13 x 17¾in): cut 1 from main fabric

fold

strap 112 x 10cm (44 x 4in): cut 2 from lining fabric

front 30 x 40.5cm (12 x 16in): cut 1 from main fabric and 1 from lining fabric

position of front inside pocket

7cm (2¾in)

front inside pocket 29.5 x 29cm (11¾ x 11½in): cut 1 from main fabric

fold

position of side pocket

side/bottom strip 94 x 10cm (37 x 4in): cut 2 from lining fabric

position of side pocket

For each pocket, mark the stitch mark at the bottom centre of the pocket. For both the front inside pocket and the back inside pocket, measure and mark the fold lines 2cm (¾in) either side of the stitch line. For the side pockets, measure and mark the fold lines 5mm (¼in) either side of the stitch line.

Glossary

Appliqué One piece of fabric being stitched to another in a decorative manner.

Armhole Opening in a garment for the sleeve and arm.

Back stitch A strong hand stitch with a double stitch on the wrong side.

Bias 45-degree line on fabric that falls between the lengthways and the crossways grain.

Bias binding Narrow strips of fabric cut on the bias. Used to give a neat finish.

Binding Method of finishing a raw edge by wrapping it in a strip of bias-cut fabric.

Blanket stitch Hand stitch worked along the raw or finished edge of fabric to neaten, and for decorative purposes.

Bobbin Round holder beneath the needle plate of a sewing machine on which the thread is wound.

Centre back The vertical line of symmetry of a pattern back piece.

Centre front The vertical line of symmetry of a pattern front piece.

Cotton Soft, durable, and inexpensive fabric widely used. Made from the fibrous hairs covering the seed pods of the cotton plant.

Cutting mat Self-healing mat used in conjunction with a rotary cutter to protect the blade and the cutting surface.

Dart Tapered, stitched fold of fabric used to give shape and contour to a sewn item.

Ease Distributing fullness in fabric when joining two seams together of slightly different lengths, for example a sleeve to an armhole.

Facing Layer of fabric placed on the inside of a garment and used to finish off raw edges of an armhole or neck of a garment. Usually a separate piece of fabric, the facing can sometimes be an extension of the garment itself.

Felt A nonwoven fabric or group of fibres matted together through heat, moisture, and pressure.

Flat fell stitch A strong, secure stitch used to hold two layers together permanently. Often used to secure bias bindings.

Freezer paper A treated paper used to store frozen foods. One side has a lightly waxed surface that will stick to fabric when ironed. It is available in some major supermarkets and online.

Hem The edge of a piece of fabric neatened and stitched to prevent unravelling. There are several methods of doing this, both by hand and by machine.

Hem allowance Amount of fabric allowed for turning under to make the hem.

Interfacing A fabric placed between garment and facing to give structure and support. Available in different thicknesses, interfacing can be fusible (bonds to the fabric by applying heat) or non-fusible (needs to be sewn to the fabric).

Jersey Cotton or wool yarn that has been knitted to give stretch.

Mitre The diagonal line made where two edges of a piece of fabric meet at a corner, produced by folding. *See also* Mitred corner.

Mitred corner Diagonal seam formed when fabric is joined at a corner. Excess fabric is cut away before or after stitching.

Notion An item of haberdashery, other than fabric, needed to complete a project, such as a button, zip, or elastic.

Pinking A method of neatening raw edges of fray-resistant fabric using pinking shears. This will leave a zigzag edge.

Pinking shears Cutting tool with serrated blades, used to trim raw edges of fray-resistant fabrics to neaten seam edges.

Pivoting Technique used to machine-stitch a corner. The machine is stopped at the corner with the needle in the fabric, then the foot is raised, the fabric turned following the direction of the corner, and the foot lowered for stitching to continue.

Pleat An even fold or series of folds in fabric, often partially stitched down.

Presser foot The part of a sewing machine that is lowered onto the fabric to hold it in place over the needle plate while stitching. There are different feet available.

Press studs Fasteners used as a lightweight hidden fastener.

PUL fabric (Polyurethane laminated fabric) A thin, waterproof fabric made by laminating cloth fabric so that it becomes waterproof on the wrong side. It is available through many online retailers.

PVC fabric (Polyvinyl chloride fabric) A synthetic, waterproof fabric with a sheen.

Raw edge Cut edge of fabric that requires finishing, for example using zigzag stitch, to prevent fraying.

Reverse stitch Machine stitch that simply stitches back over a row of stitches to secure the threads. Should be done at the beginning and end of a seam to secure it.

Right side The outer side of a fabric, or the visible part.

Rotary cutter Tool for cutting fabric neatly and easily, and useful for cutting multiple straight edges. It has different sizes of retractable blade.

Running stitch A simple, evenly spaced straight stitch separated by equal-sized spaces.

Seam Stitched line where two edges of fabric are joined together.

Seam allowance The amount of fabric allowed for on a pattern where sections are to be joined together by a seam. The distance between the raw edges of the fabric and the stitching line.

Stitch in the ditch A line of straight stitches sewn on the right side of the work, in the ditch created by a seam.

Straight stitch Plain machine stitch, used for most applications. The length of the stitch can be altered to suit the fabric.

Tacking stitch A temporary running stitch used to hold pieces of fabric together.

Tailor's chalk Square- or triangular-shaped piece of chalk used to mark fabric. Available in a variety of colours, tailor's chalk can be removed easily by brushing.

Topstitch Machine straight stitching worked on the right side of an item, close to the finished edge.

Topstitched seam A seam finished with a row of topstitching for decorative effect.

Towelling fabric Cotton fabric with loops on the surface. Also called terry cloth.

Velcro® Two-part fabric fastening consisting of two layers, a "hook" side and a "loop" side; when pressed together the two pieces stick to each other.

Wool roving A long, narrow bundle of wool fibres that have been carded, but not spun into yarn.

Wrong side Reverse side of a fabric; the inside of a garment or other item.

Zigzag stitch Machine stitch used to neaten and secure seam edges and for decorative purposes. The width and length of the zigzag can be altered.

Zip Fastening widely used on garments consisting of two strips of fabric tape, carrying specially shaped metal or plastic teeth that lock together by means of a pull or slider. Zips are available in different colours and weights.

Zip foot Narrow machine foot with a single toe that can be positioned on either side of the needle.

Index

Acknowledgments

Dorling Kindersley would like to thank the following people for their hard work and contributions toward *Made for Baby*

Crafters

Debi Birkin: Cuddly cushions, Counting sheep blanket, Cosy bath-time penguin pair, and Felt friends mobile.

Amy Cox: Button bunny.

Janet Dudley: Hanging cot organizer, Water-resistant handy bag, Set of baby bibs, Summertime booties, Sunny days bonnet, Simple summer dress, and Two-toned nappy bag.

Kathryn Meeker: Heirloom patchwork quilt, Fluttery bunting, Flower petals play-mat, Cuddly owl cushion, Folding changing mat, Anti-slam door wrap, Lovable whale, Sleepy puppy rattle, Rolling woollies, Nature-themed stacking rings, Fabric animals picture book, Squashy octopus, Flutterby pram toy, Floppy mouse toy, Safari puppets, Rosette-embellished vests, Sea-side stencilled vests, Rosette headband, Newborn cap, Newborn mitts, Tiny footprints plaque, and Cupcake gift set.

Nicola Rodway: Keepsake handprint, Decorative nursery hangers, Starry night swaddle blanket, Simple striped frame, Pretty papered building blocks, Baby gift cards, and First birthday silhouette.

Clara Smith: Fingerprint pendant.

Susan Trevor: Night-sky mobile and Fairy tale house doorstop.

Additional contributions

Proofreader Angela Baynham

Indexer Marie Lorimer

Photography assistant and hand model Carly Churchill

Additional photography Dave King

Location for photography 1st Option

Props Backgrounds

Models Teagan Dudley, William Edwards, Maddison Janice Holt, Oscar John Holt, Jimmy Knowles, Abigail Leong, Thomas Mackrill, Tulsi Nair, Blake Reeder, Saakshi Alva Roberts, Scarlet Squier, Olivia Astill-Suppria, Benedict Charles Philipson Todd, and Edward Veer